The End of the Roman Republic: The Lives and Legacies of Julius Caesar, Cleopatra, Mark Antony, and Augustus

By Charles River Editors

About Charles River Editors

Charles River Editors was founded by Harvard and MIT alumni to provide superior editing and original writing services, with the expertise to create digital content for publishers across a vast range of subject matter. In addition to providing original digital content for third party publishers, Charles River Editors republishes civilization's greatest literary works, bringing them to a new generation via ebooks.

Visit charlesrivereditors.com for more information.

Introduction

Flowers left at Caesar's grave, a tradition which still continues more than 2,000 years after his death.

Julius Caesar (100-44 B.C.)

"I would rather be the first man in a humble village, than the second man in Rome" – Caesar

Possibly the most important man of antiquity, and even all of history, was Julius Caesar. Alexander Hamilton, the famous American patriot, once remarked that "the greatest man who ever lived was Julius Caesar". Such a tribute, coming from one of the Founding Fathers of the quintessential modern democracy in reference to a man who destroyed the Roman Republic, is testament to the enduring mark that Caesar left upon the world. The ultimate conqueror, statesman, dictator, visionary, and opportunist, during his time in power Caesar expanded the borders of Rome to almost twice their previous size, revolutionized the infrastructure of the Roman state, and destroyed the Roman Republic for good, leaving a line of emperors in its place. His legacy is so strong that his name has become, in many languages, synonymous with power: the Emperors of Austria and Germany bore the title *Kaiser*, and the *Czars* of Russia also owe the etymology of their title to Caesar. His name also crept further eastward out of Europe, even cropping up in Hindi and Urdu, where the term for "Emperor" is *Kaisar*.

Even in his time, Caesar was in many ways larger than life, and because of his legacy as virtual founder of the Roman Empire, much of what was written about – and by – him during his life and immediately after his assassination was politically motivated. His successor, Octavian Augustus, had a strong interest in ensuring that Caesar's life be painted in a favorable light, while Caesar's political enemies attempted to paint him as a corrupt, undemocratic dictator who was destroying the old order of the Republic. This makes it exceedingly difficult to separate historical fact from apocryphal interjection, as the writings of Cicero (a rival of Caesar's) and the later biographies of Suetonius and Plutarch can be misleading. Nonetheless, along with Caesar's *De Bello Gallico*, his famous notes on his campaign against the Gauls, they remain our chief sources for Caesar's life – a life everyone agreed was nothing short of remarkable and changed the course of history forever.

The End of the Roman Republic provides an entertaining look at the facts and myths surrounding Rome's most famous leader and explains his legacy, which has only grown larger over 2,000 years and promises to last many more. Along with pictures of important people, places, and events, you will learn about Caesar like you never have before, in no time at all.

Bust of Cleopatra

Cleopatra (69-30 B.C.)

"Her beauty, as we are told, was in itself not altogether incomparable, nor such as to strike those who saw her; but converse with her had an irresistible charm, and her presence, combined with the persuasiveness of her discourse and the character which was somehow diffused about her behaviour towards others, had something stimulating about it. There was sweetness also in the tones of her voice; and her tongue, like an instrument of many strings, she could readily turn to whatever language she pleased..." – Plutarch

During one of the most turbulent periods in the history of Rome, men like Julius Caesar, Mark Antony, and Octavian participated in two civil wars that would spell the end of the Roman Republic and determine who would become the Roman emperor. In the middle of it all was history's most famous woman, the Egyptian pharaoh Cleopatra (69-30 B.C.), who famously seduced both Caesar and Antony and thereby positioned herself as one of the most influential people in a world of powerful men.

Cleopatra was a legendary figure even to contemporary Romans and the ancient world, as Plutarch's quote suggests, and she was a controversial figure who was equally reviled and praised through the years, depicted as a benevolent ruler and an evil seductress, sometimes at the same time. Over 2,000 years after her death, everything about Cleopatra continues to fascinate people around the world, from her lineage as a Ptolemaic pharaoh, her physical features, the manner in which she seduced Caesar, her departure during the Battle of Actium, and her famous suicide. And despite being one of the most famous figures in history, there is still much mystery surrounding her, leading historians and archaeologists scouring Alexandria, Egypt for clues about her life and the whereabouts of her royal palace and tomb.

The End of the Roman Republic chronicles the amazing life of Egypt's most famous pharaoh, explores some of the mysteries and myths surrounding her, and analyzes her legacy, which has only grown larger over 2,000 years and promises to last many more. Along with pictures of important people, places, and events, you will learn about Cleopatra like you never have before, in no time at all.

Bust of Antony in the Vatican

Mark Antony (83-30 B.C.)

"And when my own Mark Antony
Against young Caesar strove,
And Rome's whole world was set in arms,
The cause was,—all for love." - Robert Southey, *All for Love*

Mark Antony (83-50 B.C.) is one of the most unique and best known figures of antiquity, a man whose relationships with some of history's giants ensured his own legacy. A protégé of Julius Caesar's, a lover of Cleopatra's, a sworn enemy of Cicero's, and a foil for Octavian, Antony has long been remembered for the role he played in others' lives more than for his own accomplishments. Fittingly and ironically, Antony might be best remembered today for the words Shakespeare put in his mouth for Caesar's eulogy.

While Antony's relationships with Rome's most famous leaders and history's most famous woman were central components in his lives, the fact that his legacy has been intertwined with them belies the fact that he was a powerful man in his own right. Coming up as a capable and competent military man who Caesar trusted as his right hand, Antony parlayed that into governing Rome itself while Caesar fought Pompey. After Caesar's assassination in 44 B.C., Antony deftly navigated from tenuous footing as a declared enemy of the state to become one of Rome's two most powerful leaders, arguably its most powerful, in just a matter of years, outmaneuvering and getting the best of enemies like Brutus and Cicero. At the same time, Antony was notorious in his own time for his voracious appetite for vice, and the branding of him as a boor has persisted for over 2,000 years.

Of course, Antony's relationship with Cleopatra has become the stuff of legends, and one of history's most famous love stories, but even that was a byproduct of the fact that Antony ruled the eastern third of the Roman Empire as triumvir. Had Octavian and fate not caught up with him at the Battle of Actium, one of the most famous naval battles ever, history might have been very different.

The End of the Roman Republic provides an entertaining look at the facts and myths surrounding one of Rome's most famous leaders and one of history's most famous lovers. Along with pictures of important people, places, and events, you will learn about Antony like you never have before, in no time at all.

The statue known as the Augustus of Prima Porta, 1st century

Augustus (63 B.C. – 14 A.D.)

"Young men, pay heed to an old man, whom old men harkened when he was still young" –
Augustus

The importance of Gaius Julius Caesar Augustus (or as he was known from birth, Gaius Octavius "Octavian" Thurinus) to the course of Western history is hard to overstate. His life, his rise to power, his political, social and military achievements, all laid the foundations for the creation of an Empire which would endure for almost five centuries, and whose traditions, laws, architecture and art continue to influence much of Europe and the world today. Octavian was the first true Roman Emperor, and the first man since the Etruscan Tarquins, five centuries earlier, to establish a successful hereditary ruling dynasty in what had been a proud Republic for over half a millennium. He was a canny strategist, an excellent orator, a fine writer, a generous patron of the arts and enthusiastic promoter of public works, but above all he was a master politician. Octavian's great-uncle (and adoptive father) Julius Caesar was a great general, his rival Mark Antony was a great soldier, but as a politician Octavian outmatched them all.

Certainly, like all men, Octavian had his defects. Like many of the most successful politicians, he could connive, plot and prevaricate with the best of them, and he made full use of the emotional pull that his late beloved great-uncle had over the legions during the course of his rise to power. His justice was also famously heavy-handed, and he was not known for his mercy towards those he defeated in battle or marginalised political opponents. Yet despite all this, he still stands in bronze on Rome's Via dei Fori Imperiali to this day, along with the likes of Caesar, Hadrian, Trajan and Marcus Aurelius, and he is forever immortalised in all western calendars as the patron of the month of August, which was dedicated to him when he was deified, following his death, as Divus Augustus.

Like his adoptive father before him, Octavian is one of those figures whom it is difficult to know exactly what to make of, because he appears, even at a distance, to be larger than life. Yet the amount of personal correspondence and contemporary writings penned by Octavian himself, as well as his friends and associates (and rivals) is such that, when we analyse it all together, a clear picture of the man behind the bronze statue begins to emerge – the man who found Rome a city of bricks, but left her behind a city of marble.

The End of the Roman Republic provides an entertaining look at the life and legacy of Rome's first emperor. Along with pictures of important people, places, and events, you will learn about Augustus like you never have before, in no time at all.

Chapter 1: The Essence of Power – Caesar's Early Life

Bronze Statue of Caesar in Rimini, Italy

"If you must break the law, do it to seize power: in all other cases observe it." - Caesar

For a man destined to become the most famous man of history's most famous empire, the dearth of information surrounding Julius Caesar's early life and upbringing is somewhat surprising. Born Gaius Julius Caesar on July 12th, 100 BC, Caesar was the son of an ancient but minor patrician family, the Gens Iulia, who traced their ancestry back to one of the legendary founding figures of Rome, the Trojan hero Aeneas. Caesar's adopted heir, Augustus, would later commission Virgil to write the *Aeneid*. Ironically, the name Caesar would hold an imperial status across multiple continents, but the origin of the term "Caesar", technically his *cognomen* or "inherited nickname", is not precisely known, with ancient biographers ascribing it to the color of the first Caesar's eyes or the thickness of his hair (respectively *caesiis* or *caesaries* in Latin). For his own part, Caesar understandably favored a more martial interpretation, which had it that his ancestor had slain an elephant in battle.

One of the well-documented things about Caesar was that he was afflicted with what the

Romans called the *Morbus Comitialis*, a form of epilepsy, which he managed to conceal from all but his closest associates throughout his life. While the diagnosis of epilepsy comes from what was written by Suetonius and Plutarch, some historians believe the ailment may have been a byproduct of malaria, and others have speculated that he suffered severe migraines. Still others believe he suffered a different form of seizure than epileptic seizures. Whatever it was, had Caesar's debilitating ailment been made common knowledge among the Republic during his life, there's no telling how history might have been changed.

What is also known about Caesar is that he grew up in a time of relative social and political turmoil, which is saying something considering Rome's burgeoning empire was constantly experiencing turbulent volatility. Around the turn of the century, war was being waged both on the Italian peninsula and abroad, with domestic politics pitting the conservative, aristocratic *optimates* against the populist, reformist *populares*. When Caesar was in his teens, this tension ultimately escalated into an all-out war that involved him on a deeply personal level. That is because one of the leading *populares* was his uncle Gaius Marius, a military visionary who had restructured the legions and extended the privileges of land ownership and citizenship to legionaries on condition of successful completion of a fixed term of service. In the years just before Caesar's birth, Marius had waged a successful campaign against several Germanic tribes. Having earned eternal fame in the Eternal City, Marius was appointed a consul several times, but in 88 B.C. he entered into conflict with his erstwhile protégé, the optimate Lucius Cornelius Sulla (whom Caesar must also have been acquainted with), over command of the army to be dispatched against Mithridates of Pontus, an enemy of Rome and its Greek allies.

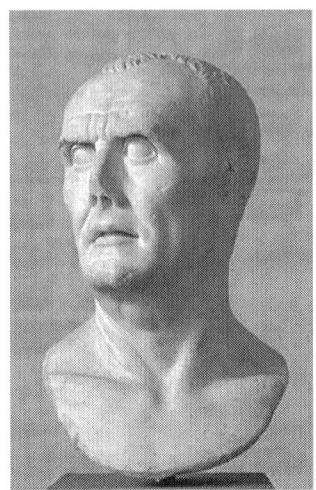

Bust of Gaius Marius, at Munich Glyptothek

Ironically, Marius's reforms had made the legions fiercely loyal to their individual generals, rather than the state, which allowed Sulla to march his army against Rome and force Marius into exile. With that, Rome's first civil war was officially under way.

Sulla's triumph proved short-lived, however. Just as Sulla departed for a campaign than Marius returned at the head of a scratch army of veterans and mercenaries, taking over the city and purging it of Sulla's optimate supporters. Though Marius died in 86 BC, his party remained in power, allowing Caesar to exploit his connection with his late uncle the following year when, at the age of 15, he was named High Priest of Jupiter, a state office of high honor. By that time, Caesar was also the patriarch of his family, with his father having passed away the previous year. It was a double responsibility which Caesar, despite his youthful age, proved more than capable of dealing with. Due to the social conventions that came with the post of High Priest, he was forced to break off a previous engagement to a relatively lowborn girl and instead take as a bride a young girl named Cornelia, the daughter of Sulla's ally Lucius Cornelius Cinna.

Bust of Sulla

Marius had reoccupied Rome while Sulla had been busy crushing Mithridates of Pontus, but with his death Cinna became the most powerful man in Rome itself. After Sulla finished mopping up the last scraps of resistance, he intended to take back Rome for himself at the head of his legions. He landed in the south of Italy and fought his way up the peninsula, defeating the armies dispatched from Rome to stop him. Some legions, including Cinna's, rose up in spontaneous revolt and went over to Sulla's side, and Cinna was murdered by his own men in the uprising. Sulla entered Rome in 82 B.C., becoming the first and only man to attack and conquer both Rome and Athens.

Upon his successful return to Rome, Sulla proclaimed himself *Dictator*, an all-powerful legislative authority which normally could be only vested in times of extraordinary crisis and never for more than a period of six months. Sulla's supporters went on a rampage across Rome, some of whom disinterred Marius's body and dismembered it before throwing the pieces into the Tiber River. Of course, the purge included the murder of Marius's most prominent supporters as well, all in an effort to allow Sulla to proclaim himself Dictator for Life.

As Marius's nephew, Caesar was a natural target of Sulla's purges, and he was stripped of lands, wealth and office. Caesar would have lost his wife too, but he refused to divorce her, earning himself a death sentence for his defiance that forced him to go into hiding. It was only the intervention of his mother's family, which included a number of pro-Sulla optimates, that managed to avert Sulla's wrath and got Caesar's death sentence commuted.

Caesar, wary of the fickle nature of dictators and no doubt sickened by what he had witnessed during the purges, decided to leave Rome and enlisted in the army, something which would have been impossible as High Priest of Jupiter; his office forbade him from touching horses, witnessing armies, or spending a night outside the city of Rome. Had Sulla not stripped Caesar of his title, the world might never have known his military genius.

Chapter 2: Antony's Early Life and Military Career

Coins depicting Antony (left) and Octavian

Mark Antony was not a great man. An extraordinary man, but not a great one, whose life was nonetheless inextricably entwined with two of the greatest men and one of the greatest women of his age. One was his mother's cousin, Gaius Julius Caesar; the other, his reluctant ally and most relentless enemy, Octavian Augustus; and the last was the love of his life, Pharaoh Cleopatra VII, Queen of Egypt. A giant Mark Antony might have been, but these, to borrow a classical phrase, were Titans.

Yet even in such exalted company, Antony did not stand wholly in their shadow. He had the makings of a great man, and had history taken a slightly different turn, he might very well be remembered as one. His courage was legendary, his battlefield acumen remarkable, and his loyalty to his friend and relative, Caesar, beyond question. Yet for all his virtue, he was in many ways a slave to vice: his appetite for women (and men, it is rumoured), his love of food, wine and debauchery, and his penchant for truly ruinous gambling all held back his advancement and, in their own way, contributed to his eventual downfall. He was a man of vast ambition, and that ambition would lead him to brush dizzying heights with the tips of his fingers, but he lacked the relentless single-mindedness and (as Napoleon would have said) the luck to seize them. For a time, his skill in battle almost led him to carve himself an Empire out of the turmoil of the Roman civil war, but it was not for this achievement that he was to be remembered.

A fine general Antony might have been, but there have been many like him throughout the centuries. His fame, which has lasted to this day, has made his name as immediately recognisable to modern audiences (if not more so) than so many Romans whose achievements were undoubtedly greater, but that fame is attributable to his storybook romance with Cleopatra, the Queen of Egypt. Their relationship has resonated so strongly in popular culture that to this day, in Italy, a man who is particularly handsome and successful with the fairer sex is known as a "pezzo di Marc'Antonio" ("A piece of Mark Antony", "like Mark Antony"). Their tale is so tragically romantic that it captured the imagination of Shakespeare himself, and it has been retold in scores of books and half a dozen Hollywood features since, growing with each telling until Antony was more a character than he ever was a person.

But who exactly was Marcus Antonius, of the Gens Antonia of Rome? Antony was subjected to Damnatio Memoriae by Octavian, so almost all images of him were destroyed and very few remain today. And much of what we know of him comes from the writings of Cicero, who detested him (and who was detested in turn) so it is hard to distinguish fact from vilification, and his status as Enemy of Rome later in his life won him no favour with Roman chroniclers either. Historians are still struggling to uncover the man behind the propaganda.

Mark Antony was born in 83 B.C., to the ancient and honourable Gens Antonia, an eminent patrician family who claimed, like most of the noble scions of Rome, to be descended from one of the Greco-Roman Gods. According to family legend, the founder of the Antonii was Anton, son of the legendary demi-god Heracles, who in turn was descended from Jupiter (Zeus). The family had a long and proud history of public service and had produced a number of highly regarded political leaders, with members of the Gens Antonia serving as consuls, quaestors, proconsuls and other important positions. Antony's grandfather, also named Marcus Antonius (as first sons of the family usually were), had served as consul and censor between 99 and 96 BC, and had been one of the most notable victims of the political reprisals of Gaius Marius, who had ordered him put to death during the purges that accompanied his return to power.

Antony's father was a far less distinguished individual, named Marcus Antonius "Creticus" ("Chalk-Man"), who was by all accounts an amiable fool. He had few means himself, for the Antonii, though one of the most respected families in Rome, had lost much of their wealth during the past few years of political reprisals, but he had married Julia Caesaris, Julius Caesar's cousin, who held the purse-strings in their relationship. This lack of personal funds did not stop Creticus from being far more generous than his finances allowed, and Plutarch recounts of how, being unable to give a friend a personal loan because his wife would not grant him any money, he called for a silver bowl to shave in and then, when his wife left the room, quickly emptied it and gave it to his friend. Naturally, he then proceeded to make himself scarce before the long-suffering Julia returned.

The young Antony seems to have had a good relationship with his father, who as the above anecdote indicates, was a kindly and well-disposed man. However, he did not spend much time with Creticus because, in 74 B.C., through the combined influence of his own and his wife's families, he was elected Praetor (military commander), a task to which (as it should have immediately been evident) he was woefully unsuited. That same year he was given imperium infinitum in the Mediterranean, essentially a blank cheque and free rein, with the objective of defeating the pirates which plagued Roman commercial and military shipping. Creticus departed for the war, leaving the young Antony behind. They would never see each other again.

Creticus spent a disastrous three years campaigning in the Mediterranean. Creticus failed to subjugate the pirates in any way whatsoever, and at the same time he also succeeded in plundering territories which had first appealed to Rome for help against the pirates, compromising a large number of alliances on the Grecian seaboard. Finally, he waged a short-lived and utterly unsuccessful war against Crete, who had allied with the pirates, and was roundly beaten for his pains. He was forced into a humiliating treaty with the Cretans (hence the mocking surname "Creticus", which also means "conqueror of Crete"), and died shortly thereafter, of illness brought on by exhaustion.

Antony, who was twelve at the time, must have taken the news of his father's death hard, and we can only speculate as to what his reaction might have been when his mother, after a remarkably brief period of mourning, re-married that same year, this time to Publius Cornelius Lentulus, that year's consul and an extremely eminent figure from the Gens Cornelia. Lentulus, who was dogged throughout his career by accusations of corruption and profiteering, seems nonetheless to have succeeded in winning over the young Mark Antony, who was extremely distraught when, in 63 B.C., Lentulus became involved in the conspiracy of Catiline. The Catiline conspiracy was one of Ancient Rome's most famous political scandals, with Catiline planning to subvert the Roman ruling body and seize power for himself and his associates. The conspiracy was short-lived, and Cicero, serving in official capacity at the time, ordered him put to death – illegally – that same year. Antony never forgave Cicero for this extra-judicial killing, even claiming later in life that Cicero had never returned his stepfather's body for burial (though this claim appears to have been fabricated), and the two were to be bitter enemies for life.

Cicero Denouncing Catiline **by Cesare Maccari**

Being raised by an amiable fool and a corrupt wastrel must have taken its toll, for it is around this time that Antony began to associate with low company, particularly the notorious Gaius Scribonius Curio, an inveterate lecher whose appetite for women, drink and gambling were legendary even among the fast set of the Roman aristocracy. Cicero, Antony's rival, later alleged that Antony had a homosexual relationship with Curio, something which, while tolerated in Rome, was not as socially acceptable as it might have been in Classical Greece, especially among the traditionalist aristocracy. However, there is no mention of any such proclivity in Plutarch's exhaustive biography, so it is hard to tell which account should be believed. Certainly Cicero had a vested interest in discrediting Antony, but he may well have been telling the truth about him and Curio.

Whatever their level of intimacy, Curio and Antony were definitely good friends, and Curio's vices set about ruining Antony, who had proven himself to be a brilliant child but quickly descended into vice and wastefulness, particularly gambling. In the five years after his stepfather's death, Antony amassed a debt of over 250 talents. It is hard to put this figure into a modern context, but roughly speaking, Antony owed between $1 million - $1.5 million dollars to his creditors. Curio, who was vastly wealthy, offered to stand surety for the debt, but when Curio's father discovered this he flew into a rage and banished Antony from his home. Antony, realising that his debt situation was quickly becoming untenable, decided that a spell away from Rome would do him good and quickly took ship for Greece, by all accounts two steps ahead of his creditors. Once there, he seems to have settled down, taking time to study rhetoric and military theory with Greek instructors, as wealthy Roman young men often did.

It was there that he first showed a remarkable amount of aptitude for both fields, with both his oratory and his tactics displaying a brash bravado which was to become a hallmark of his career as a politician and soldier. That same year, he was contacted by proconsul Aulus Gabinius, who had heard promising reports of his prowess, to join his campaign in Judaea against Aristobolus, who was fomenting insurrection there. Antony balked, but when Gabinius offered him a post as commander of an auxiliary Gaulish cavalry regiment, he accepted. The campaign against Aristobolus was brief, but Antony performed admirably in it, routing the enemy commander himself at Alexandrium and Machareus, where he was first over the enemy walls and inflicted large casualties on the vastly superior enemy forces. It was his forces, reportedly, who eventually captured Aristobolus and his son, and his excellent record in the campaign led him to have Gabinius's ear when Ptolemy, the dispossessed Pharaoh of Egypt (and Cleopatra's father, interestingly) offered the proconsul a bribe of 10,000 talents to help him regain his throne. Antony, who had discovered a new-found thirst for glory, persuaded Gabinius that a campaign with Ptolemy would be both lucrative and extremely well-received in Rome. Gabinius eventually agreed, and Antony moved forward with his vanguard and occupied the city of Pelusium, a major stronghold, whose citizens he also protected when Ptolemy, in a fit of rage, would have massacred them in reprisal.

In the ensuing campaign, Antony's conduct was exceptional. At the head of Gabinius's vanguard, he displayed both great personal valour and a keen tactical acumen, which led to Gabinius achieving decisive victory when he used his vanguard troops to outflank the enemy and strike at their rear. Antony's star was on the rise, and even his many vices were now being offset by his brilliance as a soldier, or at least excused as being in keeping with his soldierly persona. Brash, overconfident, larger than life, a prodigious drinker, womaniser and brawler, he was beloved by his men, and while some of his superiors might consider him an arrogant upstart, they recognised the power he exercised over the rank and file. His penchant for giving extravagant gifts he could scarcely afford to his friends also helped make him even more popular.

Julius Caesar

After four years of campaigning in Egypt and Judaea, Antony made the choice that was to define the entirety of his life. He accepted an offer from his mother's cousin, Julius Caesar, to join him on his campaign in Gaul and Germania. Little is recorded of his career during the course of Caesar's celebrated Gallic campaigns by his main biographer, Plutarch, but he is mentioned several times in Caesar's own De Bello Gallico, where it is stated he served as a quaestor, which could mean either that he was a staff officer or in charge of the military treasury. From Caesar's writings it appears that Antony was often in the thick of things, and he was frequently assigned command of cavalry units, displaying a particular aptitude for pursuit missions. Still, it was in politics, not warfare, that Antony was to be his kinsman's greatest asset. During the four years that Antony spent in Gaul, he and Caesar had become firm friends – it was very difficult to dislike Antony, apparently – and for his own part, Antony had developed an unswerving loyalty to his mother's cousin.

Chapter 3: Cleopatra's Early Life

Cleopatra, as shown in a contemporary bust.

In 1963, the world was fascinated by the sudden, whirlwind romance of two of its biggest film stars, Elizabeth Taylor and Richard Burton, who despite the fact that they were both married, had begun a torrid love affair. The two had met, and fallen for each other, during the filming of the Hollywood epic *Cleopatra*, with Liz Taylor in the titular role and Burton as – who else? – the gallant Roman general Mark Antony. It is a testament to what is, along with the likes of Lancelot and Guinevere and Romeo and Giuliet, one of the world's best known love stories – and all the more remarkable because it is, for the most part, true.

Yet Cleopatra's romance with Mark Antony was just the culmination of a life that was, in a great many aspects, truly remarkable in its own right. Throughout the ages she has been cast in every part: from being reviled as the personification of evil feminine wiles doing their work over great men, all the way to iconic heroine of the feminist movement. Sometimes, she has depicted as the most beautiful woman of her age, on other occasions she has been described as plain. Academics and laypeople have argued strenuously over whether she was a hopeless romantic, doomed to fall for great and charismatic men, or a ruthless politician bent on using her charms to seduce the world's most powerful figures and bend them to her will. Even her physical appearance is something of a mystery, with depictions in Greco-Roman art differing wildly from those which appear in art produced in Egypt around the time of her life and reign. Yet for all the mystery surrounding her – or perhaps because of it – Cleopatra continues to captivate popular imagination to this day, and remains one of the most iconic female rulers of all time.

Cleopatra, or as she was formally known, Cleopatra VII Thea Philopator (Cleopatra VII, Goddess, Father-Lover) was born in Alexandria in 69 BC. Her father was the Pharaoh Ptolemy XII Auletes, but because of the incestuous nature of royal marriages in Egypt, it is unclear who her mother was – it appears likely that she was another Cleopatra, Cleopatra V. Like all the Ptolemies, Cleopatra was not Egyptian. Tracing her ancestry back far enough – and indeed, not even that far – demonstrates Cleopatra was descended from minor Macedonian landed nobility and was, in effect, a full-blooded Greek without a drop of Egyptian blood in her. The dynasty to which she belonged had been established by Ptolemy, who took the name Ptolemy I Soter (Savior), a Macedonian general who had been a close childhood friend and then campaign companion to Alexander the Great. Alexander had conquered Egypt while destroying the mighty Persian empire some three centuries before, and after his death, when the wars of the *Diadochii* (the Successors) tore his empire asunder, it was Ptolemy who came to take over Egypt and establish himself there as a ruler. Ptolemy's dynasty had endured ever since, molded in the image of the old Pharaohs that the Persian Empire had long since crushed.

The Ptolemaic dynasty, like the Pharaohs of old, had a tendency to pursue incestuous inter-marriage between brother and sister, though this seems not to have affected Cleopatra in any way – all contemporary sources, whether they disliked her or not, unanimously agree that she was neither deformed or feeble-minded. However, though she suffered no disadvantages due to her birth, the environment she grew up in was hardly the most harmonious for a child. The court of the latter Ptolemies was a veritable snake's nest of plots, deceit, murder and corruption, and never more so than under the reign of the unfortunate Ptolemy XII Auletes, Cleopatra's father. Ptolemy XII's accession to the throne was marked by plotting and bribery on a grand scale, and once he was in place he grew so paranoid that, suspicious of his provincial governors, he insisted on concentrating almost all executive powers in Alexandria, where he had his seat. Such a system of government could not hope to cope with, or indeed understand, the problems faced by the Egyptian kingdom's most farspread provinces, and inevitably there were violent uprisings by those subjects at the borders of the kingdom who felt themselves abandoned to their fate. Cyprus and Cyrenaica were both lost, and other rebellions were crushed only with great difficulty and expense. At this time, Egypt had effectively become a client state of Rome – and a valued trading asset, as they provided the majority of grain imports to the capital – and, in 58 BC, despite unrest at home, Ptolemy was obliged to travel to Rome on an official visit. He chose to take Cleopatra, then just a child, with him as well, but what was meant to be a short trip ended up becoming a three-year exile: taking advantage of his absence, another Cleopatra seized the throne. It is, unfortunately, unclear which Cleopatra this was, exactly. Records from the period are sparse and not helped by the fact that the Ptolemies favored re-using the same names over and over again. She may either have been Cleopatra V, making her Cleopatra VII's mother, or Cleopatra VI, which would mean she was a sister. Either way, this Cleopatra's reign was to be short-lived – within a few months of her accession to the throne, she died suddenly under mysterious circumstances. It is highly likely that she was murdered, most probably at the hand of Berenice IV, Cleopatra VII's older sister, who took the throne as soon as she died. Berenice reigned for just under three years in Alexandria, until Ptolemy XII finally returned, at the head of a Roman army led by General Aulus Gabinius. Ptolemy had been forced to go hat in hand to Rome, having virtually no support outside of Alexandria and no chance of regaining his throne by raising armies of his own. Though this move allowed Ptolemy to recapture the throne of Egypt, he had effectively made his kingdom a vassal state of Rome, garrisoned by Roman armies, propped up by Roman spears, and dependent on Roman goodwill.

Betrayed by at least one of his eldest daughters, if not two (or his wife), Ptolemy seems to have turned to Cleopatra, his companion during his three-year exile, as his sole repository of trust. At age 14, he proclaimed her regent, a largely ceremonial position which nonetheless placed her in direct line to the throne in the event of his death. Ptolemy's reign limped on for another four years, amid further losses of crucial territory and an ever-growing dependence on Gabinius's troops, whose officers had established themselves – apparently permanently – in Egypt and promptly formed their own political faction, the *Gabiniani*, in order to try and carve themselves their own piece of the rich Egyptian pie. Finally, in 51 BC, Ptolemy Auletes died, leaving an 18-year-old Cleopatra at a nonplus. She could not assume sole rulership, for such an act would require her to get rid of her younger brother, Ptolemy XIII, with whom she was expected to share power. Cleopatra was also, in keeping with dynastic tradition, required to marry Ptolemy, who was 10 years old at the time. With the weight of tradition upon her, Cleopatra complied, but her and Ptolemy's was not a happy union. The two seem not to have gotten along as brother and sister, never mind as husband and wife, and matters were not made any easier by the fact that the gods themselves seemed to be conspiring against Cleopatra. Her rule was marked by more uprisings, and to add insult to injury, the Nile stubbornly refused to deliver adequate floods. Egypt's fertile grain fields were dependent on the periodic flooding of the Nile basin, which would coat the fields with a natural fertiliser, but a sparse flood meant even sparser harvests, which meant not only that the people would go hungry but that Egypt would be unable to deliver sufficient grain to Rome, with all the perilous consequences that entailed.

Feeling the strain, just a few months after ascending to the throne, Cleopatra effectively divorced her younger brother, whose influence was limited by reason of his age – she no longer appeared with him at official ceremonies, and started being the sole signatory on official documents, a gross breach of tradition. In Ptolemaic tradition, female co-rulers were technically subordinate to their male counterparts, regardless of whether this was actually the case, so doing away with Ptolemy was a slap in the face to the many traditionalists at court. Cleopatra may have been many things, but she was never anything but brash – perhaps even foolish. Having made enemies of the traditionalists, she promptly followed this political *faux pas* in 50 BC by upsetting one of the most powerful political factions in Egypt, the *Gabiniani*. Having been in Egypt, at a loose end, for approximately five years, the *Gabiniani* had essentially severed their ties to Rome, becoming embroiled in the civil war currently wracking the fledgling Empire in their own right.

When some exponents of the *Gabiniani* murdered the sons of Marcus Bibulus, the governor of Syria, who had been sent in friendship to request their aid in a military campaign against the neighbouring Parthians, Cleopatra saw a chance to intervene and cut the *Gabiniani* down to size. She had the assassins seized, put in chains, and delivered to Bibulus, but while this may have curried favour with the Roman governor, it did nothing to endear her to the *Gabiniani*, who promptly went from uneasy allies to sworn enemies. Cleopatra could hardly hope to rule long in the face of such massed political hostility, and in 48 BC, a plot spearheaded by Pothinus, a eunuch in the palace service, with the collusion of Cleopatra's many enemies, forced her from the throne and placed the more biddable, pliant Ptolemy XIII on it as sole ruler of Egypt. Cleopatra was a fugitive.

Chapter 4: Octavian's Early Years

Gaius Octavius Thurinus, commonly known as Octavian, was born in Rome on September 23rd, 63 B.C.. He was a scion of the Octavii, minor local aristocracy from Velletri (a town not far from Rome) who had enriched themselves through the family banking business to the point where Gaius Octavius, Octavian's father, had been able to climb the social ladder by marrying

Atia Caesonia, a member of the venerable *Gens Iulia* and Julius Caesar's niece. Although the Octavii were by no means what could be termed as patricians, they had recently made it big, so to speak, when in 70 B.C. Gaius Octavius had been elevated to the rank of quaestor and granted a seat in the Senate.

Octavian was never close to his father, who was elected praetor, an office which often required him to be away from home, in 61 B.C., two years after Octavian's birth. The following year he was dispatched to Macedonia, where he served for two years while Atia, Octavian and his two older sisters (Octavia Major and Minor, respectively) remained in Rome. On his return to the city, he died under mysterious circumstances in Nola, southern Italy, without even seeing his family again. Thus, at the age of four, Octavian was an orphan, and it fell to his mother, as well as an elderly household slave named Sphaerus, to fill the void that Gaius Octavius had left.

For the next two years they both tutored Octavian, who excelled at both Latin and Greek, as well as the rudiments of oratory that upper-class young boys were expected to learn at his age. The bond that formed between Sphaerus and Octavian during this time was so strong that he became a constant companion throughout the young boy's childhood, and later in life he would be granted both his freedom and a generous pension. After two years of respectable widowhood, Atia re-married, this time to Lucius Philippus, an up-and-coming patrician who, the following year, confirmed Atia's high hopes by securing his election as consul, and who by all accounts seems to have loved his step-children as though they were his own.

Philippus was a strong member of Julius Caesar's faction, the *populares*, who at the time were vying for political control with the oligarchic, aristocratic *optimates*. To lead the *populares* to victory, Caesar, who had already established himself as a highly successful general, had formed an alliance in 59 B.C. with the wealthy Crassus and the doughty old soldier Pompey Magnus, creating a Triumvirate of three among the most powerful men in Rome. However, in the following years, as Octavian grew into an ever more promising child, the alliance began to break apart and suffered two fatal blows when, in 53 B.C., Crassus was killed fighting the Parthians and Caesar's daughter Julia, who was married to Pompey, died in childbirth.

Pompey, who resented Caesar's ascendancy and the vastly successful campaign the younger man was waging in Gaul, began to conspire to bring about his downfall. Octavian was largely oblivious to this, however, and the following year he made his first foray into public affairs at the age of 11, when he was called upon to give the funeral oration for his grandmother Julia, Caesar's sister. His oratory was so fine, despite his young age, that report of it reached Caesar in Gaul, and he began to take a keen interest in the young boy.

Chapter 5: Caesar's Path to Consulship

"Fortune, which has a great deal of power in other matters but especially in war, can bring about great changes in a situation through very slight forces." - Caesar

Caesar may have excelled in his youth as a High Priest, but it was his military career that started him down the path to becoming an emperor, and at least before Napoleon, he was the general all subsequent generals hoped to emulate in the field.

Before he could become Napoleon's idol, however, Caesar started off his career as a common soldier. But Caesar was not a nameless face lost in the crowd. He soldiered with flair, serving with distinction in Asia and Cilicia, and after his valor during the siege of Mytilene he was ultimately awarded with the Civic Crown, Rome's second highest military decoration at the time. At the same time, Caesar appeared to grow very friendly with the King of Bithynia, Nicomedes, when he was sent on a diplomatic mission to negotiate the use of his fleet, so much so that rumours began of a supposed homosexual relationship between the two. Though Caesar always dismissed that as idle slander, political opponents continued to mock him as the Queen of Bithynia.

Meanwhile, things in Rome were beginning to change. In 80 B.C. Sulla ended his dictatorship – much to Caesar's disgust – and after having reestablished the consular offices he died two years later in 78 B.C. With Sulla gone, Caesar felt secure enough to return to the city, where he took up a highly successful career as an advocate and orator, displaying so much talent for rhetoric that it was said he might have been capable of eclipsing even the famous Cicero himself. Caesar was also noted for his body language, gesturing incredulously while pleading with a high-pitched voice.

Caesar had been a war hero, but he had not yet been a general. And he might never have been one if not for events outside his control. Having proven successful as a legal advocate, and dedicated to prove himself the best speaker the city of Rome could produce, Caesar boarded a ship headed to Greece in order to study with Cicero's former tutor. But Caesar never reached his destination; his ship was attacked by Cilician pirates and Caesar himself was captured and held prisoner on the small island of Pharmacusa.

Caesar reacted to his captivity with equanimity, displaying the cool arrogance that would become one of his defining character traits. Caesar cheerfully promised all the pirates that he would come back for them and crucify them all, a threat the pirates seem to have foolishly found humorous. Upon being informed that the pirates meant to ask for a ransom of twenty talents of silver, Caesar replied with aplomb: "Twenty? Caesar is worth twice as much, and more. Ask for fifty". The pirates accordingly did, and got them, too. What they also reaped, however, was Caesar's punishment. As soon as he was free, Caesar raised a fleet, hunted down the pirates, and personally had them crucified to the last man, as he had promised them he would do.

Following these exploits, and a daring campaign on the Roman border with Pontus which saw Caesar raise a scratch force of soldiers and repel a Pontine invasion, Caesar was elected military tribune upon his return to Rome in 73 B.C. It would be the beginning of a fairly rapid political ascent. Although several legions were employed during the following two years in crushing the revolt of the former gladiator Spartacus, Caesar appears to have played no part in the war, or at least none that was recorded. In 69 B.C. Cornelia died, possibly in childbirth, and Caesar once again departed Rome, this time bound for Hispania (Spain) where he was to serve as *quaestor*. This appointment was followed by his marriage to Pompeia (Sulla's grand-daughter, interestingly) and a string of relatively prominent political posts in Rome, where Caesar had the Appian Way rebuilt in his capacity as *aedile* and restored some of Marius' public works, in tribute to an uncle it appears Caesar cared deeply about.

In 63 B.C. Caesar allied himself with the powerful politician Titus Labienus to prosecute Gaius Rabirius, an optimate Senator, for murder. Caesar managed to defeat Cicero, who was responsible for Rabirius's defence, and this high-profile case gave him the necessary political ascendancy to run for the post of *Pontifex Maximus*, or High Priest of all of Rome. He secured his election despite accusations of bribery and demagogic oratory.

Caesar continued to be dogged by scandal when, shortly thereafter, he was accused of involvement in the Catiline conspiracy to seize power. Considered one of Rome's greatest scandals, the conspiracy included Catiline's attempt to strip the Senate of the power and eventually put an end to the Republic. The unraveling of the conspiracy, and Catiline's ultimate fate, were secured by Cicero in a famous series of speeches in the Senate, known as the Catiline Orations. In the first of the speeches, Cicero thunderously denounced Catiline while Catiline sat in the Senate, and all of the senators sitting next to Catiline slowly flocked away from him as Cicero spoke. Catiline would eventually die at the head of a small army of supporters against Roman legions, and everyone associated with his name and the conspiracy were political anathema in Rome.

Despite attempts to impugn Caesar by accusing him of being associated with Catiline, the accusations did not stick. Caesar's lifelong rival, the optimate Marcus Porcius Cato, saw Caesar being passed a note during the trials of the Catiline conspirators and, smelling treason, demanded it be read out loud. Caesar coolly complied; it was a sentimental love-letter from Cato's half-sister, Servilia, to Caesar himself. Servilia also happened to be the mother of a young man named Marcus Brutus.

In 62 B.C., in his capacity as Pontifex Maximus, Caesar hosted the festival of *bona dea*, which was prohibited to men. However, a man named Publius Clodius Pulcher ("the handsome") was caught entering the festival dressed as a woman, supposedly in order to seduce Pompeia. Despite Pulcher being acquitted – he was from a very prominent family – Caesar later divorced Pompeia, famously explaining, "Caesar's wife must be above suspicion".

Although he had climbed several rungs up the political ladder, Caesar was at another crossroads in his life. Once again, external factors influenced his next major move. At this time, Caesar was heavily in debt, a result of much spending during his time as an *aedile* and his efforts to secure his election. He turned to Marcus Licinius Crassus, an extremely wealthy patrician who was fresh off his suppression of the famous slave rebellion led by Spartacus and eventually became a part of the First Triumvirate with Caesar and Pompey the Great. Crassus' patronage helped position Caesar to be appointed governor of Hispania Ulterior. In order to maintain political office, which made him immune from prosecution for his debts, he left for modern day Spain before his praetorship expired. Caesar made this move knowing that governors were immune from prosecution, but governors also had vitally important military responsibilities via command of whatever legions were garrisoned in their territory. It would be as governor that Caesar's military career truly took off, starting with his victories over a couple of local tribes. These military successes earned him the title Imperator, the Roman equivalent of the title of Commander.

Bust of Crassus

Having been designated Imperator, Caesar once again found himself having to make a crucial decision. The title of imperator entitled Caesar to one of Rome's most famous and prestigious public ceremonies, a triumph, which would ensure his popularity and practically make him a king for a day. At the same time, however, he badly wanted to run for Consul in 59 B.C., which would require being a private citizen. Since the triumph would not come before the election, Caesar had to choose between the two, and he ultimately decided to use his newly gained prominence to run for Consul, Rome's highest magisterial position at the time.

Despite rumours of corruption, vote-buying, and pandering by virtually all the candidates involved, chiefly Caesar himself, Caesar secured his election alongside the supine Marcus

Bibulus, a long-standing optimate. Caesar himself had long since aligned himself with the *populares*, his uncle Marius's old faction. Caesar had been heavily sponsored in his run for Consul by Crassus, but now, in a brilliant stroke of diplomacy, he succeeded in reconciling Crassus with Gnaeus Pompey Magnus, Rome's powerful and vastly successful general who had made a name for himself campaigning against Spartacus, Greek pirates, and Pontus. Alongside Pompey and Crassus, Caesar established the First Triumvirate, with Crassus supplying the funds, Pompey the muscle, and Caesar the political clout necessary for governing the city. Though later triumvirates officially wielded power, like the Second Triumvirate (which formed in the wake of Caesar's assassination and included his heir Augustus and longtime general Mark Antony), this First Triumvirate acted behind the scenes to run Rome unofficially. Thus, even though Bibulus was ostensibly Caesar's equal in power, in fact Caesar utterly ignored him, at one point passing a law for land redistribution to the poor in spite of his opposition. Roman satirists referred to his time in office as "the consulship of Julius and Caesar".

Bust of Pompey

Caesar knew that the vast amount of irregularities that had marked his consulship would almost certainly lead to prosecution by his many enemies as soon as his immunity expired with his term of office. Yet again, like he had to secure the governorship of Hispania, Caesar politically maneuvered to ensure his appointment to the governorship of Cisalpine Gaul (which was not in France, as the name might suggest, but in Northern Italy), Transalpine Gaul (Southern France), and Illyricum, an appointment which also came with the command of four legions. He departed for Gaul almost as soon as his term as Consul had ended, barely a step ahead of the law.

Chapter 6: The Gallic Wars, 58-52 B.C.

Vercingetorix lays down his arms to Caesar, by Lyonel Royer (1899)

"I have fought sixty battles and I have learned nothing which I did not know at the beginning. Look at Caesar; he fought the first like the last." – Napoleon Bonaparte

In the first 40 years of his life, Caesar's political instincts had been matched only by his prodigious talent for spending money. Caesar's run as consul had left him vastly in debt, and he owed more money than even Crassus could rightly afford to part with. But as Caesar well knew, a Roman governorship was traditionally an extremely lucrative post, with the option of either taxing the province dry or leading military campaigns with the legions garrisoned there and then plundering opponents after successful battles.

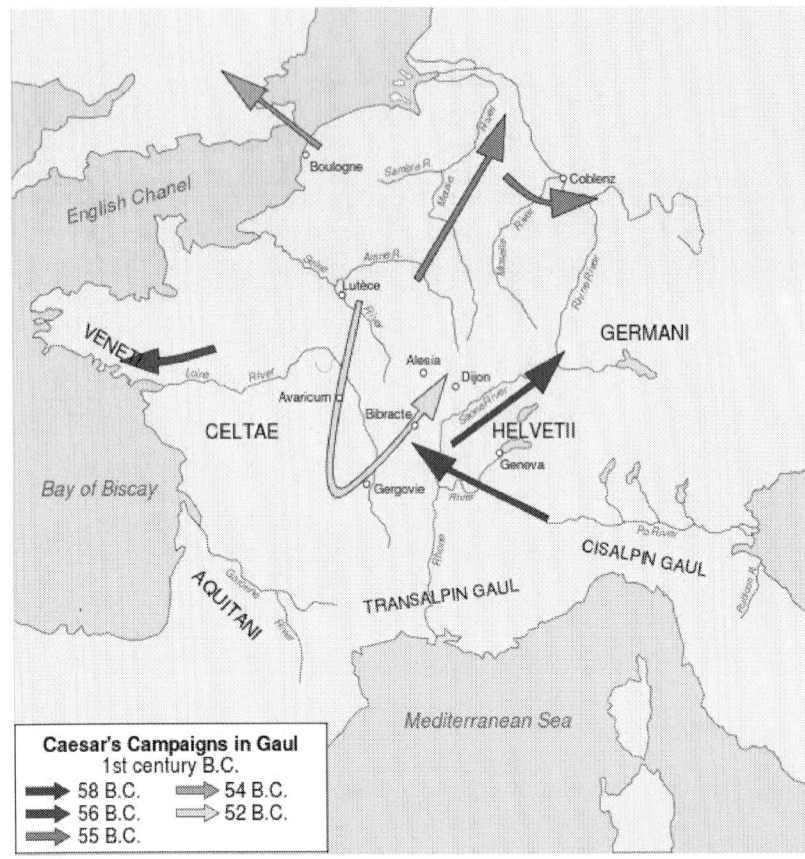

Though he had proven himself a remarkably successful statesman, as governor Caesar opted for the latter choice. His previous military experience had proven he was an excellent soldier, and he had at his disposal four crack veteran legions, the 7th, 8th, 9th and 10th, the same men that had served under him in Spain. Using the pretext that several of Rome's Gaul allies had been defeated by the Suebi, a Germanic tribe which seemed intent upon migrating south and threatening Roman territories, Caesar advanced into Gaul and defeated them. Concerned by this sudden escalation in aggression, tribes in the north began to posture for a possible war. Caesar viewed that as an escalation of hostilities and, in turn, raised two new legions and marched upon the united tribes, who were marshalling their strength in the province inhabited by the wealthy and powerful Belgae (modern Belgium).

For the first time in his career, Caesar had blundered. Emboldened by his early successes against the warlike Suebi and perhaps thinking that the tribes were far too fragmented to unite against him, he marched straight into a trap at the Sabis River, where, in 57 B.C., the allied general Boduognatus caught his legions in the open while they were making the crossing. The light footmen and cavalry, mostly members of the Atrebates, Virumandui, and Belgae, succeeded in routing the Roman skirmishers and cavalry, then turning to savage the individual Roman legions and baggage train, most of whose soldiers had been unable to arm themselves properly and were rallying around any standard they could find. Meanwhile, the heavy infantry, comprised of Nervii, had come up and succeeded in driving a wedge between the four legions that made up the main force of Caesar's army. The situation was so desperate that Caesar himself was forced to take up sword and shield to rally his troops, and he was likely only saved from annihilation by the bitter fight his soldiers put up, which allowed the 8th and 9th Legions, which had been deployed a mile to the rear with the baggage train, to reach the battlefield by forced march and relieve him.

The arrival of fresh troops turned the tide, and the Gaulish light infantry and cavalry were driven from the field by the Roman missile troops, their light armour proving no match for the hail of javelins, sling bullets, and arrows that was being hurled their way. The Nervii, an extremely warlike people, refused to retreat or surrender even when they had been surrounded, and were cut down to the last man. Caesar's use of vast arrays of missile troops, and the fact that each individual legionary was a javelineer as well as a swordsman, was instrumental in securing this and later victories, as the Gauls were typically lightly armored and did not deploy many ranged weapons.

The victory at Sabis left Caesar in control of Belgica, the province inhabited by the Belgae, and he followed this success by conquering the vast majority of what was left of Gaul in the following year, advancing with a swiftness and economy of movement which would become a characteristic of his later military campaigns. In 55 B.C., following a Germanic invasion of Gaul by a tribe who had doubtless sensed weakness in the destabilised and newly conquered territory, Caesar built a bridge across the Rhine and pillaged the territory there as an indication that further incursions would not be tolerated. That same year he led the first Romans into Britain, accusing tribes there of aiding the Gauls against him. With winter fast approaching, Caesar's forces did not make their way far into the mainland that year, but the following year, 54 B.C., Caesar's men advanced into the island's interior and conquered a large swath of territory before a revolt in Gaul due to poor harvests once again drew him back across the Channel. The Romans eventually established enough of a presence to set up the outpost of Londinium, which ultimately morphed into one of the world's most famous cities today, London.

Despite Caesar's military successes, the political situation in Rome was deteriorating. Caesar had succeeded in securing a confirmation for his posting as governor for a further five years, not least thanks to his considerable military successes, but he was growing ever more estranged from Pompey the Great, who resented the younger man's ascendancy as a general and realized it threatened to eclipse him. When Caesar's daughter Julia, whom he had married to Pompey to cement their alliance before assuming the governorship, died in childbirth, the last link between the two men was severed. And when Crassus was killed campaigning in the East in 53 B.C., the Triumvirate came to an abrupt end.

Caesar wished to return to Rome to establish his political position there, but in 52 B.C. all of Gaul rose up in arms against him under the leadership of Vercingetorix of the Avernii, who was named High King. Vercingetorix turned out to be a canny fighter who avoided open battles against the superior Roman forces, and he even managed to defeat Caesar's men in several skirmishes. Eventually, however, Caesar lay siege to Vercingetorix and his men around Alesia and, despite being attacked front and rear by Vercingetorix's defenders and other Gauls who came to try to lift the siege, succeeded in defeating them both and taking the stronghold. This effectively marked the end of large-scale resistance in Gaul and brought it firmly under Roman control.

Caesar's successful campaigns in Gaul have become the stuff of military legend, in part because he had the foresight to document them himself. Caesar wrote a famous firsthand account of the Gallic Wars, apparently from notes he had kept during the campaigns, and he wrote *Commentarii de Bello Gallico* (Commentaries on the Gallic War) in the third person. Caesar's account described the campaigning and the battles, all as part of a propaganda campaign to win the popularity of the Roman people. As a result, he left out inconvenient facts, including how much of a fortune he made plundering, but the work still remains popular today, and it is still used to teach Latin.

Chapter 7: Rome's Great Civil War, 50-46 B.C.

"The die is cast." – Caesar upon crossing the Rubicon.

By the end of the Gallic wars, the alliance between Caesar and Pompey had devolved from alliance to rivalry, and when his governorship ended in 50 B.C., Pompey was ready to gain an upperhand in Rome. In 50 B.C., with his term as governor having ended, Caesar received a formal order by the Senate, largely the product of Pompey's machinations, to disband his army and return to Rome, but Caesar was certain that he was going to be held to account for his debts and other irregularities. Assuming that any trial he participated would likely be a witch-hunt specifically designed to permanently tarnish him, he would have none of it.

In 50 B.C., Caesar would have to greatly rely upon Antony's loyalty. The great general's political troubles were coming to a head, and there seemed to be every likelihood he would be recalled to Rome and submitted to a trial by his political rivals, who were headed by Caesar's former friend and ally Pompey Magnus, who had recently been married to Caesar's own daughter (who had died shortly beforehand). Recognising that he would need a powerful voice in the Senate, Caesar dispatched Antony to Italy, to speak for him and drum up popular support for his cause. Since Caesar's political mandate was expiring, he would soon lose his immunity from prosecution, so he prepared to march into Italy to pursue what he claimed where his rights.

Caesar's claims were not exactly legitimate, but Antony seems not to have cared. Indeed, he set about defending his friend with remarkable zeal. Once in Rome, Antony re-united with his old comrade Curio, who had attached himself to the Caesarian party and had, if anything, grown even more in popularity in the years Antony had been abroad. Curio's influence, and Caesar's name (not to mention the funds Caesar endowed him with), in addition to Antony's dashing reputation as a beau sabreur and his skill at oratory secured Antony a position as tribune of the people, and also the rank of augur, which like many senior religious positions in Rome also carried significant political clout.

In his new political role, Antony was instrumental in ensuring that the optimates, Caesar's political rivals, did not do him too much damage. When he learned that Pompey was raising troops to form an army to oppose Caesar, he outmaneuvered Consul Marcellus, who was an optimate, by using his political powers to ensure that the newly raised troops, which Pompey had spent so much time collecting, were sent to General Bibulus in Syria. Thus, the soldiers of whose loyalty Pompey could be assured were dispatched to fight against the Parthians, severely limiting the optimate power-base.

Furthermore, Antony also made sure that Caesar's voice was heard in the Senate. Caesar had abandoned the larger part of his armies north of the Alps and, with a single legion, he was marching southwards to put his case personally, or so he claimed, to the people. Caesar's optimate opponents wanted he and his party, the populares, to be heard as little as possible, lest their arguments sway those among the Senators who were still undecided. To that end, they made sure that the proclamations that Caesar routinely dispatched southwards were never heard, either by the Senate or by the common people. However, vested with the authority of tribune of the people, Antony was able to read Caesar's speeches himself, and the optimates were powerless to resist him.

Clearly the situation in Rome quickly became untenable. Having crossed into Northern Italy, Caesar was encamped close to the northern bank of the Rubicon River. This was a hugely momentous event, as the Rubicon marked the southernmost boundary a general could advance on Rome from the north with his army, and the last people to infringe upon this border had been the military dictators Marius and Sulla, the memory of whose purges was still fresh in the minds of many Romans. If Caesar crossed the river in arms, it would be war. Antony found himself struggling to defend Caesar against a furious – and terrified – optimate opposition, and matters came to a head when the Senate took a vote as to whether Caesar or Pompey should stand down. The optimates wanted Caesar to disarm, the populares wanted Pompey to do the same, and Antony, seeking to pour oil over troubled waters, took the floor and proposed that both generals should dismiss their forces and meet for talks.

Many of the senators accepted this proposal, seeing a chance to be saved from civil war, but Consul Lentulus (the second of the two consuls, along with Marcellus, and also an optimate) refused to let the matter be put to a vote. He shouted Antony down, and instead proposed a motion for martial law to be instituted to counter what he called the threat of Caesar's invasion, a decree which, if passed, would almost certainly mean Pompey Magnus's appointment as plenipotentiary dictator. Antony demanded the right to use his tribune's power of veto, but Lentulus denied him, a gross infraction. Antony, furious, bellowed that he demanded to be heard, but Lentulus ordered him forcibly manhandled out of the senate. Antony fought back, and was apparently brutally beaten for his efforts, something which was also against all law and canon, as his positions as tribune and augur made it a crime to lay hands upon him. Antony sent word of what had happened to Caesar, and shortly after left Rome to join his kinsman himself, disguised as a slave.

Antony met Caesar and his men at Ariminium, where Caesar took advantage of Antony's half-healed wounds by parading him in front of his soldiers, of whom he was a fond favourite. Cynics often argue that Antony's wounds may have been exacerbated for the occasion, or even fabricated altogether, but either way they had the desired effect. Caesar pointed to Antony's illegal ejection from the Senate as proof of the fact that his optimate opponents would stop at nothing to be rid of him, and further inflamed his soldiers by pointing out the wounds Antony had sustained, crying that these were the type of brutes who would hold absolute power in Rome if he stood down. His oratory so inflamed his men that even the ones who had doubts about the legality of Caesar's actions were wholly persuaded, and Cicero was later to sourly remark that, just as Helen had brought about the Trojan War, so Antony had brought about the Civil War. It was an exaggerated remark, but it serves to indicate the importance of Antony's role in the whole affair.

Bust of Cicero

Since Caesar refused to obey the Senate, Pompey worked to have him accused of treason. Caesar, meanwhile, had taken his own initiative. After much deliberation, he decided that Antony's treatment could mean only that his opponents would never surrender peaceably, and in the spring of 49 B.C., he marched. Things finally came to a head in 49 B.C. Leaving the majority of his forces in Gaul, Caesar headed south for Italy that January at the head of the 13th Legion, despite repeated remonstrations by the Senate and threats by Pompey. That month, Caesar and his men crossed the Rubicon River into Italy, thus entering Italy as invaders, and it's likely that similar exploits by his uncle Marius and Sulla were playing in his mind. According to Suetonius and Plutarch, as his troops filed by, he famously quoted the Greek playwright Menander, remarking: "The die is cast".

With Rome's most famous civil war now having started, Pompey was assigned by the Senate to defend Rome, but he apparently felt he did not have enough forces to confront Caesar. Pompey chose to abandon the city without giving battle, citing the inexperience of his troops when compared to Caesar's veterans as his reason for retreating, despite having vastly superior numbers. Caesar formally entered Rome shortly thereafter, taking control of the city and being recognised as Dictator by the senators who still remained. It is not recorded whether Caesar met Octavian during this period, but it seems reasonable to assume he must have done so. Indeed, there is every likelihood that Octavian talked to Caesar and left a good impression with his great-uncle, for he would not be forgotten

Of course, with Pompey and his men still a threat, Caesar hadn't won yet. Caesar marched north and quickly defeated forces loyal to Pompey in Spain. He then turned south to pursue Pompey and several senators (mostly optimates) who were loyal to him, all of whom were still on the run. Pompey managed to slip away from Caesar's clutches and headed for nearby Greece, leading Caesar to cross the Mediterranean and disembark his men in Greece.

During all this, Antony remained behind in Rome. More comfortable as a soldier than as a politician, he seems to have chafed in his political work, which required him to pacify a large number of petitioners and attend scores of official functions, a business which seems to have bored him immensely. His behaviour as a politician was worsened by the fact that he had a poor memory for grievances, so when people brought him issues in need of redress, he tended to forget them altogether. Moreover, as often happened during moments of inaction (or perhaps, more simply, as always happened, but was less objectionable on campaign) he soon turned to vice, and got himself in serious trouble over his liaisons with several married patrician women. This did little to endear Caesar's faction, which Antony represented, to the aristocracy, though Antony did succeed in making himself exceedingly popular with his soldiers, with whom he shared in training, food and drink, in addition to lavishing them with gifts.

Pompey finally gave battle at Greece, quickly demonstrating why he had earned the title Magnus. The older general displayed a flash of his former self when he savaged Caesar's vastly outnumbered army at the Battle of Dyrrachium in July of 48 B.C., but one of the few who realized the extent of the victory was Pompey himself. Believing that he had not scored a major victory, Pompey refused to follow it up as Caesar retreated. Caesar himself realized it, noting, "Victory today would have been the enemy's, if only anyone among them had possessed the good sense to grasp it".

Matters might well have come to a head for Antony, for he was dangerously close to wearing his welcome thin, but following the defeat at Dyrrhachium, Caesar found himself in dire need of reinforcements. He sent an urgent message to Antony, urging him and Gabinius, Antony's old general in the Egyptian campaign, to take ship at once with as many men they could muster and join him in the fight against Pompey. Gabinius, however, wavered, reckoning that crossing the Mediterranean in winter, when it was notoriously storm-wracked, would pose too great a risk. Gabinius instead opted for an overland march, which would in all likelihood have taken far too long, so disregarding the risk, Antony raised as many troops as he could and marched to Brundisium. The port was blockaded by one of Pompey's admirals, Libo, but the advance elements of Antony's fleet were able to take to the sea and drive him off, allowing the entire army to embark on any boat they could lay their hands on, including fishing skiffs. Antony's crossing was hardly peaceful – he was pursued by Libo and, due to contrary winds, found himself with his fleet off a lee shore (in nautical terms, when a contrary wind risks pushing a sailing ship into the shallows, where it may be wrecked, with no possibility of maneuvering). However, due to a stroke of good fortune, the wind changed at the last minute and he was swept back in the direction he needed to go. As his ships sailed past the coast, he saw the wreckage of Libo's ships, which had been shattered on the rocks by the same wind which had rescued his own.

The fair winds blew Antony straight to Caesar just in time. Pompey, who had been so surprised by his opponent's retreat after Dyrrhachium that he had assumed it was a feint designed to trap him rather than a genuine withdrawal, was at last stirring himself into action and marching on Caesar's outnumbered force, which had entrenched itself at Pharsalus, in northern Greece. Caesar made Antony his second-in-command and, expecting battle, put him in charge of the right wing of his army. Despite the reinforcements, Caesar's troops were still heavily outnumbered. Caesar had around 20,000 legionaries with him, in addition to around 7,000 local and allied auxiliary troops and around 2,000 allied cavalry, while Pompey could count on between 40,000 and 60,000 legionaries, 4,000 auxiliaries, and 7,000 allied cavalry. In addition to this massive numerical advantage, Pompey also held the high ground and was well-provisioned, while Caesar was getting dangerously close to running out of supplies. Despite Antony's reinforcements, every man in Caesar's army knew (and if they didn't, Caesar made sure to tell them) that they must win or die.

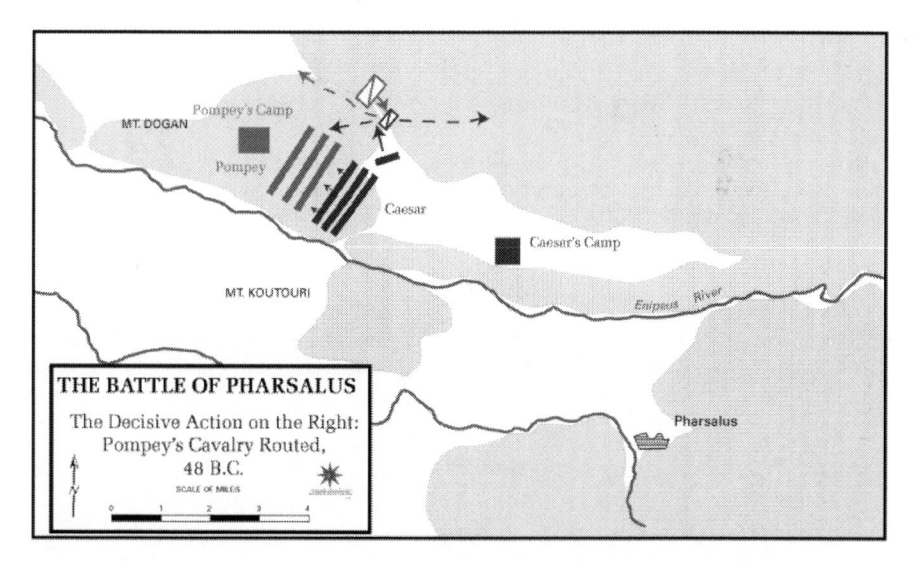

THE BATTLE OF PHARSALUS
The Decisive Action on the Right: Pompey's Cavalry Routed, 48 B.C.

Caesar advanced his men up the hill, while Pompey ordered his to stay put, reasoning that Caesar's troops would be exhausted by the time he reached his lines, but the veteran legionaries of Caesar's force paused in full view of the enemy lines and rested for around half an hour before marching onwards, without any order to do so. The two lines collided, with Antony's right holding fast while the struggle was most vicious on Caesar's left, where Pompey's cavalry was in danger of overwhelming the line, having pushed back Caesar's vastly inferior horse. Caesar, however, had bolstered his cavalry with veteran infantry, who succeeded in driving back Pompey's troops and then, striking against Pompey's open flank, rolled up his line and routed him. it was a spectacular victory, and it meant the end of Pompey's threat to Caesar. Though Pompey himself managed to escape, he would be famously murdered by Ptolemy XIII, Cleopatra's brother, whom he approached as a supplicant later that year.

The victory was so momentous that when news of it reached Rome, it allowed Caesar to be named dictator a second time, and it was around this time that he did Mark Antony the honour of raising him to the office of Master of the Horse, a highly prestigious position under the dictatorship because the Master of the Horse was effectively the dictator's second-in-command. And when the dictator was away – as Caesar was, since he immediately took ship for Egypt to pursue Pompey – it made him into the most powerful man in Italy, not to mention one of the extremely few figures whose powers of office were not suspended by the dictatorship. Thus, while Caesar proceeded towards Egypt, where he would become embroiled in the civil war between Ptolemy XIII and his sister Cleopatra, who would become his lover, Antony returned to Rome, where he set about governing Italy.

Not surprisingly, Antony's tenure as Master of Horse was no more successful than his time in politics before Pharsalus had been. He continued to indulge his immoderate appetites for eating, drinking, gambling and women, causing much grumbling among the traditionalist aristocracy, who felt his conduct was unworthy of the foremost man in Rome. Around this time he also divorced his second wife (almost nothing is known of his first, Fadia, the daughter of a freedman), Antonia Minor, after accusing her of carrying on an affair with Antony's friend, the tribune Publius Cornelius Dolabella. Of course, that Antony would divorce a woman for her infidelity is supremely ironic given his own reputation, but shortly thereafter he married Fulvia, a formidable woman who is said to have taught him the error of his ways and cured him almost entirely of his bad habits.

Chapter 8: Caesar & Cleopatra

Depiction of Cleopatra and Caesarion

Pompey's chances of winning the civil war had been lost after Pharsalus, but he managed to flee in the ensuing rout, possibly by disguising himself as a common merchant. Caesar, satisfied with his victory, returned to Rome where he was hailed as a liberator and proclaimed Dictator once again. In a token gesture, Caesar ran for Consul in what was a guaranteed victory and then resigned his dictatorship once he had secured his position – all this with his legions encamped outside the city serving as a silent but persuasive threat.

Having heard a rumor that Pompey was attempting to raise men against him in Egypt, Caesar took ship for Alexandria, only to find upon his arrival that Pompey had been murdered on the orders of Egypt's young pharaoh, the boy-king Ptolemy XIII, who thought he would curry favor by delivering Pompey's head to Caesar in a box. According to legend, the pharaoh's treatment of Pompey enraged Caesar, as Pompey's callous demise was not befitting one of the greatest Romans of the age. Caesar's relationship with his rival had always been a complex one, and he is said to have wept when Ptolemy presented him with Pompey's head. Although Caesar was there chasing Pompey's men, he quickly became involved in Egypt's own civil war. As a consequence of Ptolemy's barbarity, Caesar impulsively decided to side with his sister Cleopatra in her bid for the throne of Egypt, escalating what was rapidly becoming an all-out civil war. Egypt at the time was a client state of Rome, though not a full-fledged province, and the main provider of grain for the ever-hungry city's depots.

Utterly enraged by what he referred to as Ptolemy's casual barbarism, Caesar asserted Rome's superiority over Egypt – not to mention the fact he had an army on Egyptian soil – by installing himself in Alexandria and proclaiming himself arbiter of the dispute between Cleopatra and Ptolemy. All of this quickly reached Cleopatra, who had plenty of spies in the Egyptian court, and she realised that Ptolemy's colossal blunder was a heaven-sent chance to reassert her claim to the Egyptian throne. Already fairly certain that Caesar's new-found loathing for Ptolemy would lead him to side with her in any case, Cleopatra decided to strike while the iron was hot. She quickly travelled to Alexandria, where Caesar had taken up residence in Ptolemy's palace. At a loss as to how to actually enter the palace itself, which was heavily patrolled by Ptolemy's personal guard in addition to Caesar's own men, she finally settled upon an idea which has fascinated the world ever since. She had one of her followers, Apollodorus the Sicilian, wrap her into a carpet, hoist her onto his shoulder, and march her past the palace guards.

Cleopatra Appears before Caesar, by Leon Jerome

When Apollodorus was received by Caesar, he unrolled the carpet and Cleopatra, slightly dishevelled but otherwise none the worse for wear, appeared before the Roman general. Caesar was 52 at the time, just over three decades older than Cleopatra, who was 21, but Cleopatra might well have known that Caesar was something of a womaniser, having already conducted a famous affair with Servilia, the mother of Marcus Brutus. Be that as it may, Cleopatra chose to appear before Caesar virtually *en desabilhee*, wearing little to nothing, and most of the sources from the ancient world agree that the Egyptian queen was a famous beauty. She seduced him, by all accounts, that very night, and it seems the ever ambitious Roman eventually came away impressed by the lavish and exotic lifestyles Egypt's royalty enjoyed.

It is unclear whether Cleopatra ever truly loved Caesar – that is something that only she can ever have truly known – but she was certainly canny enough to realise the political advantages of a liaison with him. Prior to Caesar and Cleopatra's meeting, all evidence pointed to Caesar intending to do away with Egyptian independence altogether, and formally annex Egypt into the Roman dominion. However, after they began their relationship in such a spectacular fashion, Caesar promptly discarded his annexation plans and became the principal backer of Cleopatra's claim to the throne of Egypt.

Ptolemy was not prepared to take Cleopatra's sudden ascendancy lying down, however. Shortly after Caesar made his formal announcement of support for Cleopatra's claim he fled the city with most of his entourage, and raised his armies. Caesar, who had only 4,000 men with him, could not hope to fight, so for almost a year between 48 and 47 BC he and Cleopatra were besieged inside a compound within Alexandria's walls. However, the besieging force was unable to breach the compound and seems to have contented itself with attempting to starve Caesar and Cleopatra out, something which was impossible as they were able to keep their lines of communication open and resupply themselves via fortified access to the sea, which the compound possessed. In January of 47 BC, Caesar managed to get word to Mithridates of Pergamum – an ancient rival of Egypt, ever since the wars of the *Diadochii* – and request his aid. Mithridates marched with some 16,000 men, causing Ptolemy's forces to fall back. Caesar sallied from Alexandria, combined his forces with Mithridates, and marched upon Ptolemy's army.

The two armies, both around 20,000 strong, met at the Nile shortly afterwards. Caesar's veterans, the shock troops, were in the vanguard and they attacked the Egyptian troops, which were equipped as a traditional Macedonian Phalanx with heavy bronze armour, shields, and 18-foot pikes. Roman armament and tactics were superior to the Phalanx, something they had already amply proved in their conquest of Greece, and Caesar's men and their allies made short work of Ptolemy's force, instigating a rout. Ptolemy himself was caught in the headlong, panicked rush for safety, and he drowned attempting to cross the Nile. With his death, Cleopatra became *de facto* sole ruler of Egypt, with Caesar's blessing, though for formality's sake she married Ptolemy XIV, another brother, to appease the traditionalists at court. Caesar chose to linger in Alexandria for a further three months, despite his presence being urgently required in Rome. During this time, Cleopatra also gave birth to a boy, whom she named Ptolemy "Caesarion" Caesar, who she claimed to her dying day was Caesar's son, though Caesar himself steadfastly refused to formally acknowledge the boy as his.

While Caesar embroiled himself in the civil war between Ptolemy and Cleopatra, he nonetheless sent a list of people he wished to put forward for public office to Rome. Among the names was that of Octavian. At the time, Octavian was 15 and, as tradition dictated, he had been formally invested with manhood, meaning he could stand for office. Nevertheless, he was still very young for the exalted position that Caesar had nominated him for, which was that of *pontifex* (pontiff), a priest of the most important religious order in Rome. With Caesar's patronage, Octavian's election was assured, and shortly thereafter Caesar lavished another gift upon Octavian by appointing him *Praefectus Urbi* (Prefect of the City), a position which, though ceremonial, gave him a chance to mix with the political elite, to watch, learn and become known to them.

Never one for staying too long away from the action, shortly after his victory at the Nile Caesar embarked for a campaign in the Pontus, where he defeated Rome's old enemies so quickly and comprehensively that he remarked caustically that Pompey must have been an inferior general indeed to have required so long to subdue them. While he was in the Pontus, Caesar received intelligence that Cato the Younger had raised an army in Northern Africa and intended to march on Rome. Cato the Younger had a strong reputation among his contemporaries as a philosophical, moral and steadfast statesman who had long opposed Caesar and others' corruption. Having been part of the Senate group loyal to Pompey, Cato had been on the run since the civil war broke out.

By all accounts, Octavian was a sickly teenager. When Caesar was campaigning in Northern Africa in 47 B.C., he asked Octavian to join him, but poor health – and his domineering mother's intercession – prevented his going, even though it was accepted that part of a young Roman nobleman's *cursus honorum* was some form of military service. Caesar was disappointed but accepted that Octavian must safeguard his health, and even went so far as to award Octavian military decorations for the North African campaign.

Caesar quickly marshalled his forces and took ship for Thapsus, in Numydia, where he defeated Cato completely. A proud Stoic, Cato, according to the ancient patrician tradition, took his own life rather than endure the shame of defeat. According to Plutarch, Caesar's response upon hearing news of his suicide was, "Cato, I grudge you your death, as you would have grudged me the preservation of your life." A few years later, one of Cato's sons would participate in Caesar's assassination.

A statue of Cato the Younger reading Plato's dialogue *Phaedo* while preparing to kill himself.

Following his triumph over Cato, Caesar was feted in Rome, and in the following months, he took the young Octavian, who was performing admirably as pontiff, under his wing. In 45 B.C., Caesar took ship for Iberia, this time to deal with Pompey's sons, who had escaped to Spain and continued to prove troublesome. He asked Octavian to accompany him, but once again Octavian was too sick to travel.

This time, however, Octavian was determined to join his great-uncle on what promised to be his last major campaign against the *optimates*. Thus, he embarked upon a private vessel with just a few friends, including Marcus Agrippa, his future general, and sailed for Spain, but he was shipwrecked off the Iberian coast and forced to march across miles of hostile territory to Caesar's camp, a feat which is said to have greatly impressed him. Caesar succeeded in bringing Pompey's sons to battle at Munda in 45 B.C.. Despite being outnumbered almost two to one, Caesar took the offensive and attacked the enemy forces, which were commanded by Pompey's son Gnaeius Pompeius, and Titus Labenius, Caesar's onetime ally who had served under Caesar in Gaul and then later defected to Pompey's side when Caesar had crossed the Rubicon.

In its opening phases, the battle seemed to favor neither side in particular, obliging Caesar himself to join the ranks. His presence invigorated the men of the 10th Legion, which began to push back the Pompeian wing. At the same time, King Bogud of Mauritania, Caesar's ally, launched his cavalry against the enemy's rear. Labienus, the commander of the Pompeian cavalry, moved backwards to intercept them, but this led the embattled legions to think that Labienus was fleeing the field, so they broke formation and ran. In the ensuing rout, tens of thousands of them were slaughtered as they attempted to flee for safety, and all 13 of Pompeius's battle-standards, the famous Eagles, were captured by Caesar. Troops would ordinarily fight to the death to defend their Eagles, so the fact that all were taken is a clear indication of how complete the rout of Pompeius's forces was. Labienus himself was killed on the battlefield and buried with honor. With the last challengers to his utter dominion of Rome finally vanquished, Caesar returned to the city, where he was appointed Dictator for Life.

The Senate, which had been thickly staffed with Caesar's partisans and had grown increasingly servile, organised lavish games for Caesar's return to celebrate his triumph at Munda, something many Romans found to be in poor taste. After all, the battle at Munda has been against fellow Romans, led by scions of an ancient and noble house that Caesar had all but extinguished (though he had also granted clemency to a great number of his political rivals, who had since been welcomed back to Rome). It was the first sign of a growing popular disaffection with Caesar, which culminated in riots following the great triumphal games organised in honor of Caesar's other victories throughout the years. The presence of large amounts of veterans in the city, and the vast grants of land Caesar bequeathed to them, also served to irritate a significant number of the population. Although Caesar remained popular with the common people, he was beginning to lose some of their love, which did not go unnoticed among his rivals in the Senate, some of whom were already actively engaged in plotting his downfall after their hopes of a Pompeian victory in the field was dashed by Caesar's victory at Munda.

After Caesar defeated the rebels at Munda, he returned to Rome with Octavian sharing his own carriage, and the two became so close that people would approach Octavian to ask Caesar for favours, knowing the young man had his great-uncle's ear. As part of the celebrations for Caesar's latest victory, he was named consul and dictator for a period of 10 years, and granted the right to nominate new patricians, a power which he used to elevate Octavian (among others) to the utmost rank of the aristocracy. Later that same year, at Caesar's insistence, Octavian, along with Gaius Maecenas and Marcus Agrippa, his closest friends, travelled to Macedonia, where he continued his *cursus honorum* by being tutored in rhetoric and warfare.

In 46 and 45 B.C., Caesar occupied himself principally with political and social reform, rewarding his veterans with grants of land, passing laws that ensured his continuing popularity with the people (such as a restriction on the importation and purchase of luxury goods) and naming his successors. Having no male sons of his own except, perhaps, Caesarion, his bastard by Cleopatra, whom he never formally acknowledged, Caesar declared Gaius Octavius (Octavian), his nephew, to be his sole and rightful heir. This was done with the provision that, should Octavian die before him, his inheritance pass to Marcus Junius Brutus, Servilia's son. During this time, Caesar also introduced the Julian Calendar, derived from the Egyptian version, which did not follow the phases of the moon as the Roman calendar did and included the presence of an extra day in the month of February every four years. This calendar is virtually identical to the one that is still in use today and marked a fundamental shift in timekeeping, although doubtless at the time it must have been met with grumbling and confusion among the common people. To this day, the month of July is named after Caesar.

While Caesar had been away from Rome for over three years, Antony had governed the city for much of that time. Caesar and Antony kept a regular correspondence, but as the Roman aristocracy's temper with Antony began to wear dangerously thin, so did Caesar's. The two quarreled for the first time in 46 B.C., when Caesar demanded Antony pay for the property belonging to Pompey which he had taken without ever providing the state treasury the appropriate compensation. In the following months, as Antony's unpopularity rose, he seems to have grown paranoid, reacting with fright and anger to what he perceived as threats to himself and Caesar, and plots to orchestrate a return to power of the optimates. He ordered the death of scores, perhaps hundreds, of real or suspected political opponents, all in Caesar's name.

Antony's actions apparently infuriated Caesar, who knew that if Antony's unpopularity reflected upon himself, then his old friend might very well find himself ousted, and he with him. Accordingly, he ordered Antony to step down as Master of the Horse, surrendering all political powers, before he could do Caesar's faction lasting harm. Antony was furious, rightly recognising Caesar's actions as a humiliating demotion, and the two did not speak for almost two years, during which time Antony, as a private citizen, trailed at a loose end and continued to indulge in his vices. At the same time, Antony apparently stayed loyal despite his anger; he was approached at least once by anti-Caesar conspirators, but he always refused to even consider joining in any plots against his old friend. Interestingly, however, Antony is said not to have reported Trebonius, a plotter who approached him, to Caesar. Eventually the two were formally reconciled in 44 B.C., after Caesar had returned to Rome in triumph, having pacified Egypt and defeated the Pompeians and optimates in North Africa and then again in Iberia. Caesar, who was to stand for election as consul for the fifth time, nominated him as his praetor, a highly prestigious position.

When Caesar did finally return to Rome, the Eternal City was introduced to Egypt's young queen. At this point in his life, Caesar had been married to Calpurnia, who he had taken as a wife in 59 B.C., but having extramarital relationships was hardly abnormal for a powerful Roman at the time. The following year, in 46 B.C., Cleopatra visited Caesar in Rome, where he was in the process of having himself proclaimed dictator for life, much to the chagrin of his opponents in the Senate. Her visit provoked something of a scandal; foreign mistresses were all very well, and it was accepted that a Roman general might warm his bed any which way he chose when he was away from home, and heads would be politely turned the other way. It was quite another matter, however, for Caesar to openly flaunt his mistress before all and sundry, and especially before his long-suffering wife, Calpurnia, who retired into seclusion over the matter.

Several of Caesar's enemies, most notably the famous orator Cicero, were outspoken in their disgust for Caesar's relationship with the Egyptian queen, but Caesar appears not to have cared – possibly as a consequence of his growing arrogance. He appeared publicly arm in arm with Cleopatra on a number of formal occasions, and commissioned a gold-lacquered statue of Cleopatra, depicting her as the Egyptian goddess Isis, to be placed in the temple of Venus Genetrix he had personally endowed. He was canny enough, however, not to give in to Cleopatra's repeated insistences that he make Caesarion his heir, something he could not theoretically do, in any case, since Cleopatra was not a Roman citizen. Cleopatra was desperate for her son to be proclaimed Caesar's successor, but in the event <u>Caesar chose to appoint his nephew, Gaius Octavian, as his heir, with a provision that if Octavian should die before him then</u> his inheritance should pass to Marcus Brutus, his former lover Servilia's son. In the next two years, Cleopatra was often in Rome, alternating her time between there and Alexandria which, thanks to Caesar's intervention and diplomacy, was finally stable enough to allow her to leave the city for months at a time. Most of the factions who had plotted against her had been crushed, and with no other pretenders to the throne and the biddable Ptolemy XIV as her co-ruler, Cleopatra was reasonably satisfied. Barring the matter of Caesarion's succession, she could not have been happier.

Chapter 9: The Ides of March, 44 B.C.

The Assassination of Caesar, by Karl Von Piloty (1865)

"I have lived long enough both in years and in accomplishments." - Caesar

It appears as though Caesar planned to make Octavian his second-in-command for a grand campaign against the Parthians, for there is every indication he would have made him Master of the Horse (a position previously occupied by Mark Antony, and essentially the dictator's second-in-command) and given him command of the five legions stationed in Macedonia for the invasion.

However, this was never to be. Caesar had just finished a remarkable 6 year period that saw him go from enemy of the state to absolute power over the greatest empire in the world. During these same years, however, dark shadows were gathering over Caesar, though he refused to acknowledge them or even to admit to noticing them. Hubris, it seemed, had finally taken Caesar in its grasp, and he remained intentionally or unintentionally oblivious to the enemies plotting behind his back. Despite warnings from Mark Antony, his wife Calpurnia, and many other members of his inner circle, he continued about his business while his enemies sharpened their knives.

Caesar surely knew he had enemies; with a political career such as his, what man wouldn't have? However, he clearly underestimated just how much his ascendancy had begun to alienate some of the optimates and former Pompeians in the Senate and among the Roman aristocracy.

Perhaps, having seen Sulla's relatively untroubled time as Dictator, he believed he could replicate the older man's feat. Perhaps he was simply pleased by the honors bestowed upon him by the panderers among the Senate and was unaware of their true feelings. Be that as it may, Caesar willingly or unwillingly made his presence at the head of the Roman Empire intolerable to many people.

Tensions began to rise in the wake of Caesar's triumph and victory games, which had already been marred by accusations of being in poor taste and overly lavish, when Roman mints began producing coins in honor of Caesar that featured his effigy upon them. This was a highly unusual practice, because effigies had generally been reserved for the dead. In many minds, such behavior smacked dangerously of monarchy, and the mutterings against Caesar increased.

Caesar also did himself no favors when he tolerated the behavior of some of his more overly enthusiastic supporters who, during a speech he gave in the *Rostrum* (the public orator's platform in the Forum), placed a laurel wreath on a statue depicting him, an honor properly reserved for Gods and Kings. When two tribunes had the wreath removed, Caesar had them both stripped of their office, a move which angered many of the conservative optimates who held Republican institutions to be sacred.

Despite these acts, Caesar still moved somewhat cautiously. Though he might have welcomed signs of adulation from the crowd, he took care to distance himself from any notion that he wished to be acclaimed as a king. When, on a different occasion, the crowd cheered him by shouting *"rex, rex, rex"* ("king, king, king") at him, he quieted them. Nevertheless, with each passing day, Caesar's opponents were becoming certain that, having dispatched all his rivals, Caesar planned to re-establish the monarchy. When Antony, in what appears to have been a blunder (although the event might have been staged) offered Caesar a diadem, a symbol of royalty, during the Luperchalia festival of February 15th, 44 B.C., Caesar made a great show of refusing it, possibly to show how earnest he was in his desire not to revive the monarchy.

However much he tried to distance himself from any notion of royalty or being a king, there was no denying the fact that Caesar, as Dictator for Life, was effectively wielding absolute power, a fact which did not escape many of his rivals or, for that matter, supporters attempting to advance themselves. One such man was Lucius Cotta, a rather servile individual who had the brilliant notion to actually petition the Senate to bestow the title of King upon Caesar, who was preparing plans for an invasion of Parthia, of which it had long been prophesied, "only a King will conquer her".

No matter what Caesar did or how he actually felt, the damage was done, and the events of the Luperchalia persuaded his enemies to act. At some point in 45 B.C., complaints and grumbling gave way to conspiracy. The Roman Senate consisted of between 800-900 members, and a group of around 60 of them, who called themselves *Liberatores* (Liberators), began meeting in secret with the intent of plotting Caesar's assassination. These conspirators were led by Gaius Cassius

Longinus and – most famously – by Marcus Junius Brutus. Brutus, who had been named second in line to Caesar's inheritance in Caesar's will and was the son of Caesar's onetime lover Servilia, is an enigmatic figure: his motives for heading a conspiracy against a man who at one time could almost have been considered his adoptive father have never been especially clear. Some suggest that he felt slighted that Octavian was named Caesar's heir in his stead, and others point to the deteriorating relationship between the two, because Brutus had aligned himself against Caesar and sided with Pompey during the civil war. There is even a suggestion that Servilia, who had grown estranged from Caesar, planted the notion in her son's head due to jealousy over Cleopatra, and there's almost no doubt Brutus envisioned himself fulfilling a destiny similar to the famous ancestor who had expelled the last king from Rome.

Brutus

Whether it was one or a combination of these factors, Brutus seemed to consider Caesar's assassination necessary to defend the Republic against any form of monarchy that might arise. And Brutus was not interested in idle speculation: planning quickly became concrete and, after a number of secret meetings in various locations across the city, the *Liberatores* determined that Caesar would be killed on the floor of the Senate House, the most symbolic place for such an act.

Caesar appears to have had no inkling of what was coming, but on the evening before the Ides, Antony was enjoying a quiet dinner at home when he was approached by Servilius Casca, one of the Liberatores who was having a change of heart at the eleventh hour. Casca was vague about the details of what was going to happen, but he must have let slip enough to alarm Antony.

According to Virgil, the dawning of the Ides of March of 44 B.C. (March 15th) was greeted by great portents across the breadth of the Roman dominions: the volcano of Etna is said to have erupted prodigiously, great flocks of crows were seen in the ominously dark skies above Rome, while the Alps were shaken by earthquakes, the "voices of the Gods" thundered above the German forests, and animals spoke in human tongues. No doubt Caesar, a level-headed man, would have dismissed all this talk as arrant nonsense, but what most Roman historians are adamant about is that his inner circle was replete with foreboding that morning. Rumors of an attempt on Caesar's life by the *Liberatores* had filtered through to Caesar's supporters, and Calpurnia begged him not to go to the Senate that day, virtually throwing herself at his feet in her worry. Caesar might have been swayed by his wife's misgivings, if nothing else in order to humor her, but for the intervention of Brutus himself. It is said that he took Caesar by the arm and, smiling, pointed out to him how absurd it would be if the Dictator of Rome were to not show himself in the Senate for fear of the ravings of a woman half-deranged with worry for her beloved husband. This swayed Caesar, who accordingly left for the Senate as he had originally planned.

That morning Antony hurried to the Senate, where Caesar was due to give a speech, hoping to convince him to stay away. However, on his way there he was intercepted by Trebonius, who managed to delay him long enough for the conspirators to attack Caesar. Had Caesar's long time protégé reached him, who knows how things may have gone that day, but the two men were prevented from meeting.

Morte di Giulio Cesare **("Death of Julius Caesar"). By Vincenzo Camuccini, 1798**

When Caesar entered the Senate House, he was approached, as arranged, by a *Liberator* named

Tillius Cimber, who presented him with a petition for the cancellation of the exile of his brother, who had been banished some time previously. Caesar ignored him and brushed roughly past, but Cimber seized hold of his robe, half-pulling his toga from him. Caesar snatched his toga away from Cimber, demanding "What is this violence?". It was at this point that Servilius Casca, who despite his confession to Antony had decided to go along with the plot after all – doubtless in fear of what the other *Liberatores* would do to him if he got cold feet – attacked. He also seized Caesar by his robe and, drawing his dagger, dealt the Dictator a glancing cut to the neck. Casca was no assassin, and the cut seems to have been trivial, so much so that Caesar, who had doubtless seen worse on campaign, turned and seized him by the neck, snarling "What are you doing, you wretch?". Casca panicked and, dropping his dagger, screamed "Help me, brothers!". His desperate entreaty broke the paralysis that had seized his fellow *Liberatores*, with upwards of 60 men descending upon Caesar. The Senators were not military men, which was made clear by the haphazard manner in which they stabbed Caesar with knives and daggers. Caesar, stabbed multiple times, tripped and fell to the ground, where the conspirators continued to savage him. Despite the fact Caesar was stabbed nearly two dozen times, doctors concluded only one of them was a fatal wound.

As with all of history's decisive moments, the assassination of Caesar has taken on a legend of its own, and popular perception of the murder is often rooted more in colorful myth than reality. The most enduring myth about Caesar's death is that his last words were "Et tu, Brute? (Latin for "And you, Brutus?), but this is almost certainly apocryphal. Both Suetonius and Plutarch, which still remain the main sources for Caesar's life, report that he said nothing. Instead, they wrote that as Caesar lay dying on the Senate House floor, he caught sight of Brutus among his murderers and, rather than face this betrayal, he drew a part of his robe over his head.

Jean-Léon Gérôme's painting of Caesar's assassination

The majority of the *Liberatores,* terrified by the implications of what they had done, fled the scene, as did most of the Senators, who doubtless feared their presence would be taken for involvement. Caesar's body lay unattended for three hours before anyone came to attend to it, while Brutus and Cassius marched through the city center, proclaiming to all who would listen that Caesar's tyranny had come to an end and that Romans were free again. The conspirators quickly learned that their cries were mostly falling on deaf ears. Terrified of the threat to the peace that the vacuum of power caused by Caesar's demise would doubtless cause, most Roman citizens had locked themselves indoors as soon as they had gotten wind of what had happened.

Antony, who was just outside the Senate House when the murder was carried out, heard the screams and cries of horror from within and, realising what was happening, fled in a panic. He did not know exactly what had happened inside the Senate, but he could guess: Caesar, his kinsman and closest friend, was dead, and everything was about to change. It is reasonable to assume that when Antony heard the screams from inside the Senate House, he expected to be killed as well. After all, he may have been more hated than Caesar among the conspirators and their supporters, and in the wake of Caesar's assassination, Antony fled the city dressed as a slave.

Cleopatra, who was in Rome at the time, also felt compelled to flee for her life. She took shelter in Alexandria, devastated by Caesar's death, and secluded herself in mourning.

Cleopatra, as shown in a contemporary Egyptian statue.

Caesar's death was also a crushing blow for Octavian. Not only had he lost the closest thing he had ever had to a father, he had also been stripped of his most powerful political protector and his main source of advancement and influence. Ignoring the entreaties of his friends, who begged him to take command of the Macedonian legions, Octavian sailed for Italy at once. He was still just 19.

Octavian as a young man, in military dress.

Chapter 10: The Second Triumvirate

Octavian vs. Antony

A tetradrachm coin depicting Cleopatra

Octavian landed in Italy to find a land riven by uncertainty and fear in the wake of Caesar's death. It is reasonable to assume that when Antony heard the screams from inside the Senate House, he expected to be killed as well. After all, he may have been more hated than Caesar among the conspirators and their supporters, and in the wake of Caesar's assassination, Antony fled the city dressed as a slave. He returned shortly afterwards, however, when the liberatores assured him there would be no purges following Caesar's death. He took over as consul, as precedent dictated, and on Cicero's advice, following a speech his rival gave in the Senate, he agreed to order an amnesty for all of Caesar's murderers.

While he outwardly displayed peaceable intentions towards the liberatores, in his mind Antony was plotting revenge against the men who had killed his dearest friend. When the time came to deliver Caesar's eulogy, before thousands of assembled citizens, Antony asked for the floor.

Since everyone knew how close the two had been, Cicero, Cassius and Brutus could hardly deny him. What followed was a masterpiece of crowd-pleasing rhetoric, in which Antony, seizing Caesar's bloody and torn toga, harangued the mob, pointing out each murderer from among the assembled Senators, naming and shaming them one by one. As Antony had expected, the mob was so incensed by his speech that they began howling for the liberatores's blood, forcing them to flee the city that night as their houses were attacked. This seminal moment in Antony's life has been forever immortalized by Shakespeare himself, whose dramatic account of Antony's eulogy ("Friends, Romans, countrymen, lend me your ears; I come to bury Caesar, not to praise him.") is still widely invoked today.

Antony was firmly entrenched when Octavian arrived in Italy, but to everyone's great surprise, Caesar had changed his will before he died, making Octavian his sole heir, granting him the rights to two thirds of his fortune, and his name. Octavian promptly changed his formal name to Gaius Julius Caesar, dropping the lowborn Octavius from his name.

Octavian now needed funds if he was to have any political clout. The garrison that Caesar had amassed at Brundisium in preparation for the Parthian expedition defected to him as virtually a matter of course, for he was Caesar's confidant and, for all intents and purposes, his son. In a daring stroke, knowing the country was in disarray, Octavian seized the war treasury that was meant to pay for wages and supplies for the army at Brundisium, a sum amounting to hundreds of millions of sesterces, and began making his way north, intercepting a tribute payment shipment along the way and appropriating that as well. He continued northwards towards Rome, persuading more of Caesar's veterans, dispersed in garrisons throughout the country, to join him. By the time he arrived outside the city gates in early May of 44 B.C., he had more than 3,000 men with him.

Octavian's arrival on the scene caused a shift in power, as he was directly challenging Mark Antony for supremacy within the Caesarian party. Everyone knew that Mark Antony had been Caesar's oldest and dearest friend, but Octavian was the dead dictator's heir apparent and confidant. Ultimately, it boiled down to the desirability of the two candidates: Mark Antony, whose excesses were well known, found it easy to make friends among the populace and rank and file, but tended to alienate the aristocrats whose support he needed, while young, soft-spoken, unassuming Octavian both lacked Antony's offensive brashness and possessed a (false) air of innocence which many wily politicians thought they could take advantage of. Accordingly, the *optimate* Cicero, who had been among the architects of Caesar's murder, began to deliver a series of vicious speeches against Antony, who saw public opinion slowly begin to turn against him.

As his year in office (and his immunity from prosecution) drew to a close, Antony persuaded himself of the wisdom of leaving Rome, particularly as Octavian was continuing to amass troops, and decamped for Cisalpine Gaul, where he was to assume governorship after ousting the *liberator* Decimus Brutus. Before he left, he suffered the indignity of losing two legions, through a mixture of bribery and exortation, to Octavian.

Antony travelled northwards but encountered opposition from Decimus Brutus, who stubbornly refused to give up his governorship, forcing Antony to besiege him at Mutina. It was the biggest chance of Octavian's career thus far, and he did not let it slip. While Antony was preoccupied with Decimus Brutus, Octavian persuaded Cicero – who thought Octavian easily manipulated - to have the Senate denounce Antony as an Enemy of Rome, declaring his wars and consulship illegal. Two new consuls, Aulus Hirtius and Gaius Pansa, were elected, while Octavian himself, who as Caesar's heir had succeeded in drawing a large number of his veterans to his banner, was granted imperium to defeat Mark Antony.

Accordingly, Octavian set off northwards, alongside Hirtius and Pansa, the two consuls for 43 B.C., and their own consular troops. His troops met Antony's at the Forum Gallorum, near Mutina, in April of that year, in an inconclusive engagement which saw Antony's troops withdraw, but also led to Pansa's death. The two sides met again in a far more decisive engagement six days later, on the outskirts of the city of Mutina. The battle was close-fought, with Octavian himself, in the thick of it, reportedly holding up the eagle battle-standard of one of his legions when the standard-bearer was killed, but eventually Antony was driven from the field. However, in the fighting consul Hirtius was also killed, meaning Octavian now had control over the entire army.

Forming the Second Triumvirate

The Senate, however, did not react kindly to a new Gaius Julius Caesar, encamped in northern Italy with his own private army. The lion's share of honours for the victory at Mutina went to Decimus Brutus, who had done little to deserve them, and the Senate also demanded Octavian transfer command of his legions to Brutus, something which he was far from ready to comply with. Instead he defied the Senate, stubbornly staying put and, to add insult to injury, refused to attack Antony. It is likely he made overtures to the defeated general around this time, for he also demanded the Senate reverse their earlier decree naming him an enemy of the state. When they declined, he marched his army southwards and forced them to comply before standing for election as consul for 43 B.C., alongside one of his relatives. Several months later, Octavian met in Bologna with Antony and Marcus Lepidus, one of Caesar's most loyal generals, and the three of them instituted a second Triumvirate which would divide power between them. The Triumvirate, unlike the first one, actually had a legal basis, and was meant to last for five years, being legitimised by popular vote.

Coin depicting Lepidus

The reasons for this alliance, uneasy though it was – there is every indication that the two men heartily disliked each other, thinking of one another as a drunken braggart and an upstart, respectively – was simple: the enemy of my enemy is my friend. From their exile in the Middle East, Brutus and Cassius had succeeded in raising an army large enough to threaten Rome herself. The Second Triumvirate (the first having been Caesar, Pompey and Crassus, some years previously) banded together with the express intention of hunting down and destroying Caesar's assassins.

One of the first acts the Triumvirate carried out upon seizing power was to reintroduce the old Sullan custom, which Caesar had famously found morally repugnant, of proscription. People subject to proscription were branded enemies of the state, their property forfeit, and they themselves executed unless they promptly decamped abroad. Proscription was meant as an emergency measure to protect the Republic from enemies within in times of crisis, but obviously it leant itself to abuse, since there was no form of trial required.

The Triumvirate used it almost exclusively as a way to rid themselves of political opponents, as well as replenishing their coffers by having wealthy men proscribed. Sources dispute what role Octavian had in this, with some arguing that he was foremost in ordering the executions and others that he attempted to quell the excesses of his two fellow Triumvirs. Certainly, Octavian was quick to forsake his alliance with Cicero, who Mark Antony gleefully had put to death, putting an end to an enmity which had begun during Antony's childhood. To say Antony and Cicero hated each other would be an understatement. Cicero constantly wrote critically of Antony's behavior in Rome, and when Cicero delayed one Senate session, Antony had threatened to burn down his house. But now Antony got the upper hand, literally. After Cicero was hunted down by Antony's and Octavian's forces, he was decapitated, and Antony ordered that Cicero's heads and hands be displayed publicly in the Forum. By the end of the proscriptions, between 150 and 300 Senators had been put to death.

In addition to purging enemies, proscription flooded the state treasury with gold, enough to raise as many as 28 legions which, in the spring of 42 B.C., they shipped to Greece to fight Brutus and Cassius, the two leading *liberators*, who were still at large and had succeeded in building a vast army for themselves, going so far as to ally with Rome's old enemy, Parthia. Octavian was flush with success at the time, having recently succeeded in having Caesar deified by the Senate, which made him, in turn, *Divi Filius* – "son of a God" – a fair step upwards from son of a minor provincial aristocrat.

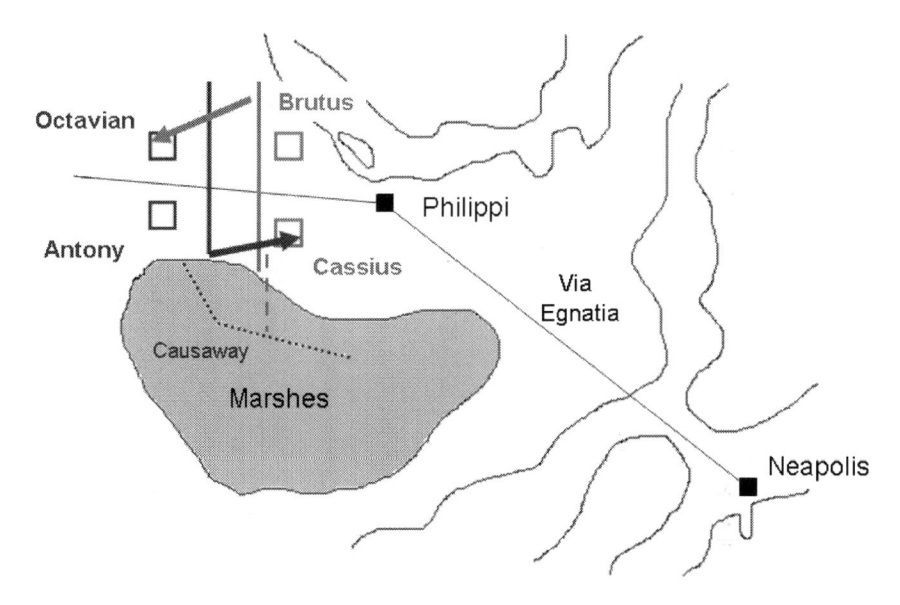

In autumn of 42 B.C., Antony and Octavian's armies encountered those of Brutus and Cassius in a double engagement near the town of Philippi, in northern Greece. It was a colossal battle that lasted several days and involved almost half a million soldiers, a fight on a scale seldom seen in antiquity, and it was a resounding success for the triumvirate. The two sides first clashed in early October of 42 B.C., with Antony's troops squaring off against Cassius's and Octavian's facing Brutus's. Antony drove Cassius back, but Octavian was almost overrun by Brutus. However, Brutus could not let Cassius be destroyed and so retreated rather than completing Octavian's defeat. Cassius, hearing a false rumour that Brutus had been defeated and killed, committed suicide. The two sides drew back and caught their breath, and three weeks later battle was joined again. This time Brutus was soundly beaten, and he killed himself rather than accept defeat and humiliation. The rest of their armies surrendered, leaving Antony and Octavian masters of the field. Antony took the lion's share of the glory, as his troops had been in the thick of the hardest fighting – with Antony himself at their head. Octavian, who was wary of battle, had delegated the command of his men to Marcus Agrippa.

Antony and Cleopatra Unite

Despite their momentous victory, the Triumvirate was beginning to show some serious cracks in its foundations. Though their alliance was politically convenient, Antony and Octavian continued to detest each other. Antony had never forgiven Octavian for usurping his place in Caesar's affections in his final years, and Octavian was still furious that Antony had withheld the funds he needed when Caesar had died. Both were open in their criticism and slander of each other, so to prevent the Triumvirate dissolving, an administrative division was agreed upon. Octavian would take Rome and the West, Lepidus Northern Africa and Iberia, and Antony Egypt and the East.

In 41 B.C., in his official capacity as governor of the East, Antony summoned Cleopatra to his seat at Tarsus. Apparently, his reason was to question her with regards to some funds she had allegedly supplied to Cassius, though she had stayed staunchly anti-liberator during the course of the latest civil war. Another reason for the meeting was that Antony intended to wage war against the Parthians, Rome's age-old enemy in the East, and to do so he needed the logistic and financial support of Egypt. Or perhaps he wanted a better look at the woman who had seduced his friend. Since she had often been in Rome, he would probably have met her formally, or even earlier, at Alexandria, but there was no sign of romance between the two prior to 41 B.C., when the flame that would set the Roman domains afire once again was first lit.

Whatever the reason for their meeting, the two had a whirlwind romance during the winter of 41-40 B.C., and Antony was so captivated by the exotic queen's demeanour that he spent most of that time in her palace in Alexandria. That their relationship was far from platonic was well known, as she bore him two twins, Alexander Helios and Cleopatra Selene, later that year. Be it as it may, Cleopatra presented herself before him at Tarsus in the winter of 41 BC, arriving with all the pomp and circumstance that a queen of Egypt could summon. Like Caesar before him, Antony fell for her – or was seduced by her – almost on sight. Antony himself was so captivated by her that he chose to spend the remainder of the winter and the spring of 40 BC in Alexandria with her, exciting scandal in Rome not just as a consequence of their liaison – Cleopatra had been the mistress of Antony's closest friend, after all, and Antony had a wife, the Roman aristocrat Fulvia – but because, taking advantage of Antony's power in the east, Cleopatra had her sister Arsinoe murdered. Arsinoe, who was Cleopatra's one surviving sibling, was likely more than familiar enough with her other siblings' fates, and as the last one standing she had taken refuge at the temple of Artemis, in Ephesus (Greece), which was under Antony's jurisdiction. Arsinoe claimed the right of sanctuary, but that hardly stopped Antony's henchmen, who dragged her onto the temple steps and butchered her, thus removing once and for all the last credible threat to Cleopatra's throne. This elicited great scandal in Rome, where the right of sanctuary was held to be sacred, and Octavian, who was at odds with Antony, wasted no chance to use the story to discredit him.

By now, the Triumvirate was beginning to show some serious cracks. Antony was forced to break off his tryst with Cleopatra and head to Rome when he discovered that his wife Fulvia, who had stayed there, was struggling to contrast a smear campaign launched by Octavian. Thus, in late spring of 40 B.C., Antony abruptly cut his relationship with Cleopatra short. Whether he feared the relationship would utterly condemn him in the eyes of the mob, or he felt guilty over the predicament of his wife Fulvia, who despite the rumors concerning him and Cleopatra's liaison – or possibly disbelieving them – was steadfastly campaigning on his behalf against Octavian, is unclear. What is certain, however, is that the relationship between Antony and Cleopatra, however brief, had been intense. Nine months later, Cleopatra gave birth to twins, Alexander Helios and Cleopatra Selene, who could only be Antony's children. Quite what Cleopatra made of Antony's abandonment, however, is unclear. In all likelihood, she was fairly confident he would be back – he had a war against Parthia to prosecute, after all, for which Egypt would be an ideal base, and her seat in Alexandria was the wealthiest city in Antony's new domain.

Though Octavian had secured control over Rome and the Italian peninsula, his position was no bed of roses: to begin with, he had to find a means of disposing peacefully of hundreds of thousands of veterans – both his own men and those who had surrendered to him. There was little land (the traditional reward for veterans of the legions) available, so in the end Octavian was forced to dispossess the inhabitants of 18 towns, forcibly evicting them to make room for his soldiers. It was an unsavoury choice, but he could not afford tens of thousands of discontented soldiers wreaking havoc throughout Italy.

The political fallout from Octavian's decision was significant. While his rival Antony installed himself in Tarsus, where he began an affair with Caesar's old mistress, Cleopatra, before moving with her to Alexandria, Octavian entered into conflict with Lucius Antonius, Mark Antony's brother, and with his wife Fulvia, whose daughter he was married to but publicly – and scandalously – divorced. Antonius and Fulvia raised an army against Octavian, supposedly to protect Antony's rights, but their support among the legions quickly dwindled when the money they had promised failed to materialise. Fulvia and Antonius ended up bottled in at Perusia, which Octavian finally captured in 40 B.C. He exiled Fulvia to Sycion, but decreed a pardon for Antonius and his men, though he was not so accommodating for their political allies. More than 300 senators were proscribed and put to death for supporting Antonius, and the town of Perusia was virtually razed to the ground, though its citizens were, for all intents and purposes, blameless.

Shortly after the sack of Perusia, Octavian briefly married Scribonia in an attempt to gain further political leverage, but their marriage was so short-lived that when she gave birth to their first child some 14 months later he had already divorced her, in order to take Livia Drusilla, the daughter of a prominent patrician, to wife instead. Livia would be a dutiful wife for the rest of Octavian's life, though she may be most memorably associated with the conniving,

Machiavellian character in the famous novel and televisioin series *I, Claudius*, in which Livia seemingly poisons everyone, including Caesar Augustus, to secure her son Tiberius's succession.

Bust of Livia

Meanwhile, the Triumvirate was once again in danger of collapse, with Antony heading for Italy with an army to pursue his rights and get his wife released from her captivity. Antony was forced to break off his tryst with Cleopatra and head to Rome when he discovered that his wife Fulvia, who had stayed there, was struggling to contrast a smear campaign launched by Octavian. Fulvia died in 40 B.C. as Antony was making his way back. Seeing a chance to patch things up with Octavian, Antony agreed he would remarry, to seal the alliance that would keep the crumbling triumvirate alive, at least for a time. Accordingly, later that year he married Octavian's own younger sister, Octavia Minor, as Pompey Magnus had once married Caesar's daughter, to preserve the unity of the first triumvirate. And while back in Rome, Antony spent some time there planning an invasion of Parthia, which had supported the liberators and taken advantage of the civil war to invade some of Rome's eastern domains.

It was at this time that the Parthians, apparently sensing weakness, advanced eastwards, conquering large swathes of Syria and Judaea, which were essentially Antony's backyard. Capitalizing on the renewed goodwill engendered by his marriage with Octavia, Antony convinced his fellow triumvir Octavian to provide him with an army and sufficient supplies, and set off for Parthia to drive the enemy's forces from his domains and then, if all went well, to march into the Parthian heartland itself. However, Antony detoured to Greece on his way, where he scandalized Roman public opinion by proclaiming himself the incarnation of the god

Dionysus, displaying a foreshadowing of the penchant for gluttony which would come to haunt his and Cleopatra's final days. Meanwhile, Octavian had re-routed the army he had promised Antony to Sicily, where a rebellion by one of Pompey Magnus's sons was underway. Despite attempts by Octavia to patch things up between her husband and her brother, in 38 BC Antony decided that Octavian would never truly support his Parthian venture and so, in disgust, he abandoned his wife and children in Rome and set sail for Alexandria.

Having resolved his problems with Antony for now, Octavian might have hoped for a few months of peace to catch his breath, but it was not to be. A new threat to stability emerged, in the form of Sextus Pompeius, one of Pompey's sons, a renegade general whose establishment of a power-base in Sicily the Triumvirate had tolerated. Pompeius began preying on shipping, denying Rome vital grain supplies and forcing Octavian to act. In 39 B.C., he reached an agreement with Pompeius, who was now virtually lord of the Mediterranean, Sardinia, Corsica, Sicily and the Peloponnese, but their relationship quickly deteriorated as Pompeius continued to act as a pirate. War was inevitable, so in 37 B.C. Octavian renewed his alliance with Antony, and the triumvirate, for a further five years. Antony sent Octavian more than 100 warships, which proved to be instrumental at Naulochus, where Agrippa destroyed Pompeius's navy completely. Pompeius, stripped of his power, was forced to flee, but Lepidus, whose troops had helped Octavian secure the victory, took advantage of the chaos following Naulochus by attempting to claim Sicily, a notoriously rich island, for himself. Octavian, however, was able to suborn Lepidus's troops with promises of money and an end to fighting, and they deserted him *en masse,* leaving him in an exceedingly awkward position. This ill-judged move allowed Octavian to expel Lepidus from the Triumvirate, gaining control over his dominions.

Meanwhile, relationships between Antony and Octavian were once again heading downhill at an alarming rate. The ships Antony had provided Octavian with had been granted in exchange of a promise for 20,000 men to fight in the campaign Antony was preparing against Parthia, but Octavian ended up sending only 2000. Rebellion in Sicily meant the soldiers Antony wanted were diverted there, prompting another furious quarrel between Antony and Octavian. Only Octavia's intervention managed to pacify the two men, who reluctantly signed a treaty renewing the triumvirate for another five years at Tarentum in 38 B.C.

Even Octavia's diplomacy could not reconcile the two men, however. Despairing of ever receiving troops for his venture, Antony abandoned Rome in a black fury later that year, leaving behind Octavia, who was carrying his second child. He made straight for Egypt where, despite his having been a widower, a husband and a father in the two years since he had seen her last, he immediately resumed his amorous relationship with Cleopatra, a grave insult to Octavian's sister, and one which he was publicly furious about..

It appears that Cleopatra took her erstwhile lover's return in stride, and there appears to be no doubt that the couple happily reunited. With her trademark impulsiveness, Cleopatra pledged

Antony the money he needed to fund his Parthian expedition from the Egyptian royal treasury, and Antony married Cleopatra, according to Egyptian customs, later that year – Octavia's presence in Rome being conveniently forgotten. Antony then left Cleopatra behind and marched to war, achieving some notable initial successes in Judaea in 37 BC, where he installed Herod on the throne. He then marched on Parthia, but his campaign proved to be a catastrophe. A full quarter of his 100,000-man army was lost to disease, desertion and battle, and Antony was unsuccessful in subduing either Parthia or Armenia, being forced instead to limp back to Cleopatra with his tail between his legs. Meanwhile, as Antony struggled in the east, back in Rome Octavian had dismissed Lepidus, the third member of the Second Triumvirate, and assumed sole power over his domains

After Antony limped back to Alexandria and Cleopatra's arms, Octavian trumpeted the news of his defeat throughout Rome, reviling Antony in the choicest terms and pointing out that not only was he going dangerously native, he was also consorting with a foreign harlot while he had a fine patrician wife of the noblest Roman blood waiting for him at home with his children. Octavian's public relations offensive blamed Antony's recent failure and the consequent loss of Roman life on the wrath of the gods for Antony's sins.

Antony and Cleopatra, however, seem to have been unconcerned with Octavian's threats, or the growing popular resentment with Antony that Octavian was fomenting in Rome. It seems quite likely that Antony simply did not care any more and just wanted to be left alone in his Alexandrian idyll with the woman he loved. Like Caesar, Antony was fully charmed by the quixotic and exotic Egyptian lifestyle, and he immersed himself in it even more than his famous mentor. Despite repeated demands from Octavian that he return to Rome immediately to answer for his ill-conduct, Antony remained happily in Alexandria, and waged a new campaign against the Armenians in 34 BC, this time achieving success and annexing the territory to his and Cleopatra's domains.

At the height of their glory, the star-crossed lovers made the blunder that would change the course of history. Cleopatra organised a lavish, Roman-style Triumph in Alexandria to mark Antony's successful conquest, during which Antony's children (now numbering three) by Cleopatra were all granted royal titles in the East, Cleopatra herself was named Queen of Queens and ruler of the East, and crucially, Cleopatra's son Caesarion was named King of Kings, ruler of Egypt and the East, living God, and above all – Caesar's formal sole son and heir, thereby by default disowning Octavian in the eyes of the East. Additionally, Antony officially declared his alliance with Octavian over, proclaiming that from then on the East was free and independent of Rome.

The Donations of Alexandria, as this ceremony was called, were greeted by frosty, dangerous silence from Rome. The expiration date of the Triumvirate came and went quietly in 33 BC, with no talk of a renewal, and Antony divorced Octavia in 32 BC, declaring her unfaithful and

Octavian himself a fraud, while Octavian responded by accusing him of waging illegal wars. The following year, the war began.

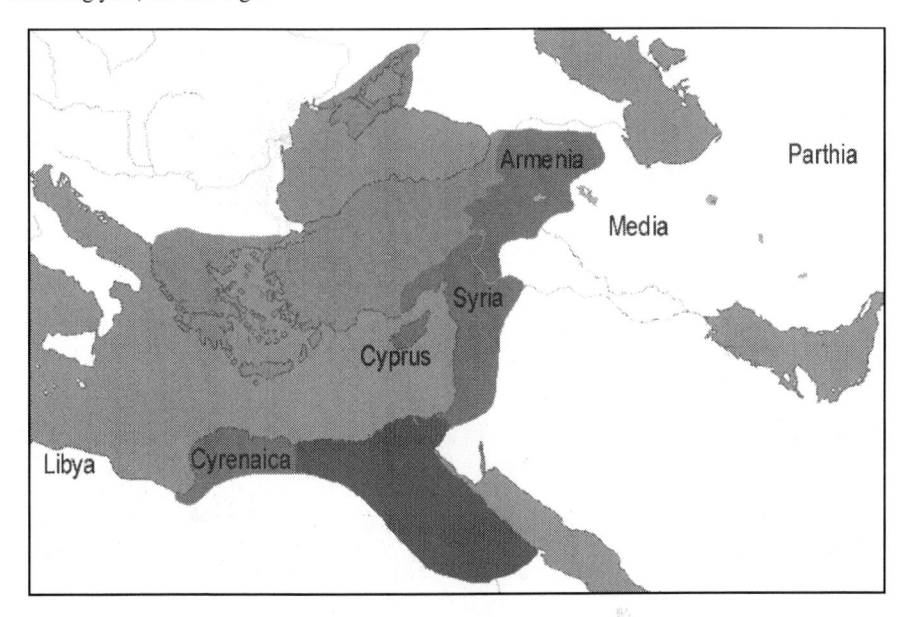

The Donations of Alexandria

Chapter 11: Rome's Third Civil War

Antony and Cleopatra, by Sir Lawrence Alma-Tadema (1883)

Between 33 and 32 B.C., relationships between Rome and Alexandria steadily broke down. In Egypt, Antony and Cleopatra accused Octavian of not being Caesar's true heir, pointing out that Caesarion was Caesar's actual son, not his nephew, and thus the worthier man to bear his name – a dangerous statement for Octavian, whose main source of public support, especially with the legions, was their love for his deceased adoptive father. Antony also unilaterally divorced Octavia, disowned his children by her, and threatened to stop the grain supply to Rome, while Octavian demanded Antony answer for waging war on Parthia and Judaea without the Senate's consent. Utilizing public relations yet again, Octavian made accusations of outright treason, while infuriating the Roman mob with tales of the excesses that the no-longer-Roman Antony indulged in within Cleopatra's palace.

In 32 B.C., Octavian declared war against Cleopatra, rather than Antony, a calculated move intended to ensure the Romans did not feel he was continuing the legacy of the fratricidal civil war. Perhaps Octavian overestimated his support, for Cleopatra and Antony were delighted to discover that both consuls and a full third of the Senate had decamped from Rome and defected to their side wholesale. The royal couple met the defectors in Greece, and for a while felt so secure in their position they even considered an invasion of Italy itself.

However, once the war began in earnest, things quickly went from bad to disastrous. In 31 B.C., Octavian's forces set sail for Greece, and the legions there immediately went over to his side, spurred by the veterans in their ranks who had once fought for his adoptive father Caesar. Both Cyrenaica and Greece fell to Octavian, essentially without a blow struck, and Cleopatra and Antony were forced to retreat back to Egypt, where they rallied the Eastern navies and prepared to contest Octavian's passage across the Mediterranean.

When Antony, with Cleopatra aboard his royal flagship, moved to counter Octavian's advance by sea, he succeeded only in getting himself boxed in at Actium, off the coast of Greece, by Octavian's numerically inferior fleet of smaller, more agile craft. On September 2, 31 BC, Antony and Cleopatra found themselves in a tactically disadvantageous position, facing Octavian's navies off the coast of Actium, in Greece. With the risk of being bottled up and surrounded at Actium by Octavian's naval forces a very real possibility, Cleopatra advised Antony to give battle, although it appears the Roman general thought victory was unlikely. Antony and Cleopatra appeared, to the untrained eye, to have the advantage: their fleet numbered over 500 vessels, almost half of which were giant five-decked quinquiremes, ramming warships that carried full-blown siege engines on board, while Octavian had only 250 far lighter craft.

However, the sea was rough that morning, favoring Octavian's more maneuverable ships, which were less affected by the rolling swells, and to make matters worse, Antony's fleet had been wracked by disease, meaning that many of his mighty quinquiremes were undermanned. The giant craft were ponderous to begin with, but without the requisite number of rowers and fighting men, they could never hope to achieve proper ramming speed. Octavian's lighter, more agile craft, filled with veteran sailors, were able to dance around the ponderous quinquiremes, showering them with hails of fire arrows, ramming and boarding where they could, and sprinting away before the heavier craft had a chance to bring their rams to bear. As the day wore on, it became more and more apparent to Antony and Cleopatra, on their twin flagships, that the battle would be lost. More and more of their craft were being sunk, scattered or overwhelmed, and still more were burning down to the waterline, their skeleton crews being insufficient to man their battle stations and extinguish fires at the same time.

As one of Rome's most famous battles, the Battle of Actium has taken on a life of its own in popular memory. One of the longest-held myths about the battle is that Cleopatra, sensing defeat, began to sail away from the fight in the middle of the day, and the lovestruck Antony followed her with his own ship, abandoning his men in the middle of the fight. While that popular myth would be in keeping with explaining Cleopatra's irresistible charm and magnetism, contemporary accounts of the battle do not suggest it was actually the case. As night approached, Antony and Cleopatra spotted a gap in the now thoroughly jumbled enemy line, and ordered their ships to speed through it without delay, making for Alexandria with all speed and abandoning their entire navy to its fate. Only 60 of Antony's ships, less than a fifth of his original strength, survived. It was a crushing blow, for Octavian and his generals had virtually annihilated Egypt's seaborne power, and Antony's with it.

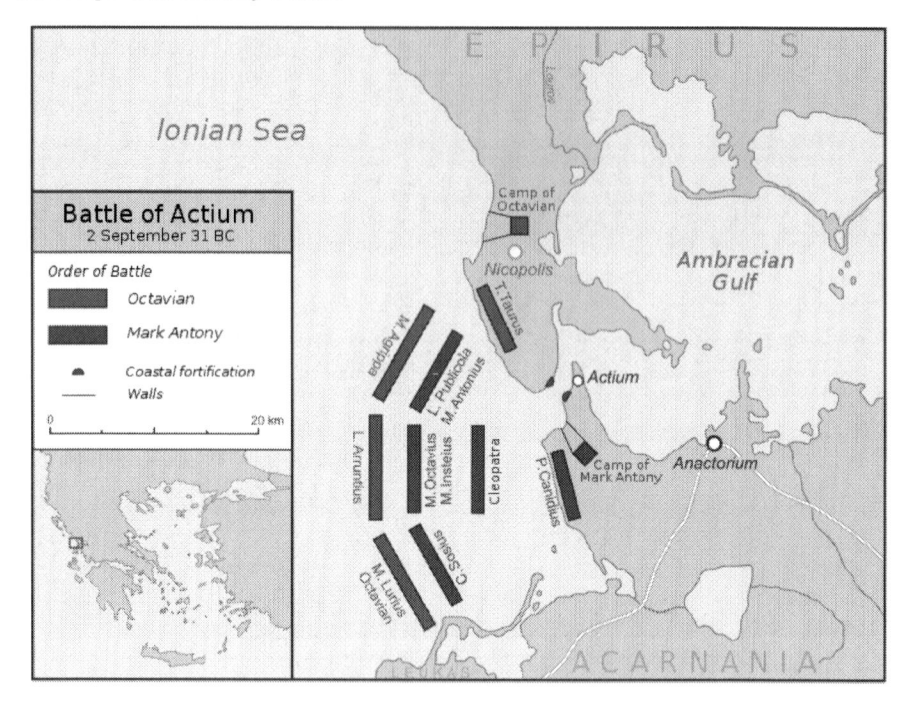

17th century depiction of the Battle of Actium

Chapter 12: Deaths for the Ages, 30 B.C.

Actium was the decisive battle in the civil war between Antony and Octavian, but Antony and Cleopatra's troubles were far from over. They retreated to Alexandria, and Antony was still fairly certain he could give Octavian a run for his money on land – he was a famous, veteran commander, after all, and he had at his disposal 19 legions of infantry and more than 10,000 cavalry. However, due to a combination of disgust over his callous abandonment of his navy at Actium, a strong sense of loyalty to Caesar and his heir Octavian (and a healthy dose of common sense, in all likelihood), in August Antony's army deserted *en masse* and went over to Octavian virtually to the last man, leaving Antony and Cleopatra stranded in Alexandria, with just their personal bodyguard for defence, at the mercy of Octavian. Antony, furious at his army's betrayal, flew into a rage and raved against Cleopatra, declaring that she had betrayed him to Octavian in hopes of saving herself. Cleopatra was so terrified for her life that she locked herself away in her private rooms, and sent a message to Antony saying that, because she believed all hope was lost, she had taken her own life.

With Octavian at his gates, Antony despaired, and his despair turned to horror when it was reported to him that Cleopatra had killed herself rather than let herself be captured, as must inevitably happen. It remains unclear whether the false rumor was a callous act, deliberately engineered to drive Antony to commit suicide himself, or if Cleopatra was genuinely distraught and not thinking clearly. Whatever the case, Antony was so overwrought that he could see no other recourse than doing what any true, noble Roman would do in the event of his defeat - fall upon his sword. However, Antony botched the attempt, giving himself a deep but non-fatal wound to the stomach. He laid himself down upon a couch, hoping that blood loss would carry him off, but as the blood flow slowed and the wound grew ever more painful, he began to beg for the release of death. Hearing of his plight, Cleopatra was horrified at what she had done, and commanded he be brought to her. Even in in his death throes, Antony was so happy to hear that she was alive that he consented, even though this required his being winched through a window, as Cleopatra had barricaded herself in her quarters. He died shortly thereafter, in her arms.

Cleopatra was so distraught over the note which had caused Antony to suffer such a painful and drawn-out death that she tore her clothes off, ripping at her hair and beating and scratching herself in her despair, before managing to achieve a measure of composure. She was captured by Octavian while praying over Antony's corpse, but though she was placed in the care of trusted men, Cleopatra would not suffer the final indignity of being paraded through the streets of Rome before the howling mob.

As everyone now knows, Cleopatra famously took her own life, and the manner of Cleopatra's death has been debated for millennia, shaped in popular memory by everyone from Shakespeare to Hollywood. Ancient historians wrote that she had a venomous snake, most likely a cobra, concealed in her private apartments, and that when she realised that escape was impossible, she provoked it into administering a fatal bite on her arm. Today most people unfamiliar with those accounts believe that Cleopatra had an asp bite her on the breast, which was how Shakespeare depicted it in his famous play. Stories differ as to what snake was used (the term "asp" is most likely a generic name for any venomous snake, but Egypt is renowned for its deadly King Cobra) and if it was kept deliberately or came to be there by accident. Some historians even argue that there was no snake at all, and that Cleopatra poisoned herself with hemlock, as Socrates had done. Still others claim Octavian had her killed, which seems contrary to the widely-assumed belief that Octavian intended to parade her as a captive through the streets of Rome in a triumph.

***The Death of Cleopatra* by Reginald Arthur, 1892**

The tragic fates of history's most famous lovers are well known, but their deaths had long-lasting effects. Cleopatra VII, Thea Philopator, was the last of the Ptolemies. Her line, which had lasted approximately three centuries, was extinguished with her. Her son Caesarion was almost certainly murdered soon after her death on the orders of Octavian, as all trace of him mysteriously disappears from the historical record, so the dynasty that Alexander's general had founded in the wars of the *Diadochii* came to an abrupt end.

Octavian quickly took advantage of his victory by having Caesarion and Antony's eldest son quietly assassinated, but he scored a propaganda victory by also pardoning most of Antony's soldiers. After Antony's death, he was subjected to damnatio memoriae, ("damnation of the memories") by Octavian, and ironically it was Cicero's son, Cicero Minor, who had the satisfaction of announcing Antony's death to the Senate. Almost all images of Antony were destroyed within the Empire, the reason so few busts of Antony survive today.

With the death of his last fellow Triumvir, Octavian was now *de facto* master of Rome.

Bust of Octavian, circa 30 B.C.

Chapter 13: Caesar Augustus

Stabilizing and Securing the Empire

Augustus with the Civic Crown.

Augustus was the most powerful man in Rome, but he now found himself caught between a rock and a hard place. For all intents and purposes, he was the uncontested ruler of Rome, but he could not proclaim himself as such, because of the risk of alienating the people, and his rivals who saw in him another Caesar. On the other hand, even if he had wished to step down, he could not do so without creating a colossal power vacuum which would almost certainly destroy Rome.

After decades of strife, Octavian intended to oversee a process of stabilisation. Three years after his victory at Alexandria, in 27 B.C., Octavian undertook what later became known as the First Settlement. During the intervening three years, there had been relatively little strife, both civil and external, and Rome was beginning to return to the way of life it had enjoyed prior to the Civil War. Thus, to prevent appearing as a despot, Octavian made a formal show of returning control over the provinces and the army to the Senate, although this was a largely symbolic gesture, as Octavian was certain that he would command the loyalty of the legions no matter who led them. Octavian also still held a number of official titles in the state which granted him a host of powers, and he hardly needed the revenue from conquered provinces, as the fortune he had amassed first as a Triumvir and later when his troops sacked Alexandria was nothing short of immense: he was doubtless the richest man in Rome, and the second barely even came close.

The Senate rewarded Octavian for his formal surrender of power by awarding him two titles, *Princeps* and *Augustus*. *Princeps*, though the root of the English word "Prince", did not carry royal connotations; it was generally used to refer to a sort of "first among equals", as the holder of the title was as often as not the most senior Senator, but could also be awarded for extraordinary services to the Republic (as it had been, some years previously, to Pompey Magnus). *Augustus*, on the other hand, was a religious title, but still symbolised a certain degree of authority. Octavian thus became *Princeps* (sometimes *Imperator,* the title given to successful generals) *Gaius Iulius Caesar Augustus, Divi Filius* (son of God).

Nor were his powers entirely ceremonial. In 27 B.C., the Senate, concerned about instability in some of Rome's provinces, asked Octavian to take direct control of them, something which he was happy to do, accepting a mandate for ten years for direct administration of Egypt, Cilicia, Cyprus, Gaul, Hispania and Syria, while the Senate retained control of Greece, Macedonia, Illirya and Northern Africa. This radically altered the balance of power in Octavian's favour, as he now controlled the greater part of Rome's domains directly, and also commanded over 20 legions, while the Senate could muster at most five from their territories, should they ever get it in their heads to oppose him. This system also allowed Octavian to cultivate the loyalty of key senators by dispatching them to important provinces as his surrogate governors, whereas the Senate chose their governors by election and changed them on a yearly basis.

Gone, it seemed, were the days of Senatorial opposition, when Caesar's addition of a backrest to his consular chair had sent senators into paroxysms of rage because they claimed he had changed his chair into a throne. Octavian was forced to outright refuse insignia of power such as sceptres, diadems and purple robes, offered by sycophantic senators eager to win favour with him, but he accepted the placement of oak and laurel wreaths, as official decorations, on his home. This had significant symbolic value, as the wreaths were generally reserved for generals during a triumph and victorious athletes. However, as the years passed, many of Rome's prominent politicians began to realise that the honours, titles and duties they had heaped upon Octavian had made him a far more powerful man than Caesar ever was. Moreover, Octavian had begun treating his nephew, Marcus Marcellus, as an unofficial heir, a political decision which was causing a strain even with Livia, his wife, and Maecenas and Agrippa, his oldest and closest friends.

In 23 B.C., Augustus fell so grievously ill that it was widely assumed, including by Augustus himself, that he would die. Augustus made arrangements for the title of *Princeps*, and some if its attendant powers, to pass onto Agrippa when he died, but he relinquished control of public finances and the legions in the provinces he administered (nominally, at least) to his co-consul for that year, Calpurnius Piso. It is reasonable for us to assume that no matter what, the legions would follow Agrippa, since he was a popular general and he would have been seen to have been named as heir by Octavian. However, despite being at death's door for weeks, Octavian eventually began to get better and, within several months, had made a full recovery. His brush with death, however, had exposed his desire for a monarchical succession, so in order to avoid any scandal later in 23 B.C. he stepped down as consul, in what is known as the Second Settlement.

However, this did nothing to curb his power, as he acquired proconsular powers instead, and was *de facto* able to exercise his will over all other proconsuls as well. That same year, Octavian was also granted the powers that came with the rank of Tribune (though not the rank itself) and that of Censor. This meant that he was now legally able to convene the Senate at will, propose motions, veto them, choose members of the Senate, examine laws to see if they were appropriate (and veto them if not), supervise public morality, select Senators, preside over any election and take the floor whenever he wished during public assemblies. In effect, Octavian had lost literally none of his authority by stepping down as Consul – in fact, he had probably gained a considerable amount. This behaviour was a hallmark of Octavian's political career: he would appear to make concessions, seeming to have a genuine desire to revert Rome to its original Republican state, while managing to actually amass ever more power.

Nor did his appointments stop coming. Later that same year Octavian was given *imperium* over Rome itself, meaning all troops within or around the city, normally under the control of the consuls, were now under Octavian's orders. By default, this now made him, in addition to his other powers, the generalissimo in control of *every single* Roman army. No one had ever amassed so much power in Rome since the monarchy, but, bizarrely, the people seemed not to mind: when, in 22 B.C. (and again in 21, 20 and 19 B.C.) Octavian, as he had promised the Senate, avoided standing for election as consul, the people became so concerned that they rioted, claiming the Senators were attempting to force Octavian out of office. Indeed, they even went so far as to refuse to let more than one consul be elected, so that Octavian could take the consulship if he wished – further proof of the fact that stepping down as consul was probably the best thing Octavian ever did for his political career. Certainly the fact that Octavian used his own private funds to engineer a colossal rebuilding project in 20 B.C. for Roman monuments, roads and public buildings, as well as paying for the grain dole out of his own pocket on several occasions, did much to endear him to the plebeians, but it is still remarkable how readily they accepted his supremacy.

There's no question that it required an unmatched political cunning for Octavian to go about consolidating so much power so quickly without making waves, but Octavian's ascendancy did not go unchallenged. In 22 B.C., he narrowly averted a crisis by appearing at the trial of Marcus Primus, proconsul of Macedonia, even though he had not been called as a witness. Primus was accused of waging illegal warfare against Thrace, using Macedonian troops, which under the terms of the First Settlement were in Senatorial control. Primus defended himself by accusing Octavian of having given him his orders, something which would have meant that Octavian's carefully constructed façade of lack of complete dominion over Rome would have collapsed like a house of cards. It later transpired that the order had been given by Marcellus (then deceased), Octavian's erstwhile heir apparent, indicating that Octavian would have been guilty of monarchical dispensation of powers to his heirs. But thanks to a heartfelt speech at the trial, Octavian was able to persuade the authorities of his innocence, and Primus was sentenced on charges of illegal warfare.

Nevertheless, the prosecutor, Lucius Murena, was unconvinced, and the following year he joined a conspiracy led by Fannius Caepio to murder Octavian. The conspiracy was quickly discovered, however, and the men involved were prosecuted by Octavian's stepson Tiberius, tried and condemned to death for treason *in absentia* before being discreetly arrested and executed, causing scarcely a ripple. Thus, Octavian deftly averted another potential crisis.

Bust of Tiberius

In 19 B.C., Octavian was also invested with all consular powers, though not the rank of Consul. He was allowed to wear Consular insignia, and sit with the two (indeed, above the two) consuls before the Senate. At this point, Octavian had appropriated virtually all the powers of the half-dozen most important political figures in the Republic (though it's even arguable whether Rome could be called a Republic at this point anymore), even though he technically *did not hold any of their offices* – something which would have raised an outcry, and in all likelihood never been allowed. Thanks to this masterpiece of political process, Octavian had come to control Rome without the majority of its people ever noticing, or caring. Later in his life he would add the titles of Supreme Pontiff and Father of the Country to his roster, but for all intents and purposes, his powers were at their peak. Though he is remembered today as the first Roman emperor, Augustus was never even referred to as an Emperor during his lifetime.

Military and Political Expansion

Map of the Roman Empire at Augustus's death. Yellow is for territories already controlled by Rome before he took power. All territories in green represent regions conquered by Augustus's generals. Pink is for client kingdoms.

Though Augustus is remembered chiefly for his stellar political career, the military expansion that took place under his auspices was almost as remarkable. The above map gives an idea of the scale of his achievements, and though his generals were active prior to 19 B.C. it was mostly after that year, when his political position was most secure, that the drive for Augustan expansion began.

In 19 B.C., the Cantabrian tribes of Spain, who had long resisted Roman incursions, were finally crushed, incrementing Octavian's private finances and filling the state coffers with the gold from their extremely productive mines. Three years later, the lawless region of the Alps was added to the bag, serving as a springboard for an invasion of Pannonia, Illirycum and the

Germanic region of the Rhineland in 12 B.C., spearheaded by Octavian's two stepsons by Livia, Tiberius and Drusus. The campaign in the Rhineland, despite the notorious loss of three entire legions at the Battle of Teutoburg Forest, was successful, and Drusus pushed the Roman boundaries as far north as the Elbe before dying during the campaign in 9 B.C., removing him from the running as an heir apparent.

Later Years and Succession

In his later years, Octavian began to gradually withdraw from public life, placing ever greater emphasis on his children and stepchildren and testing their mettle as he attempted to determine which one was the most deserving of taking his place. By then, the Romans had begun to take for granted that, once Octavian died, there would be a genuine succession. In the end, despite some friction, Octavian selected Tiberius (officially Tiberius Julius Caesar Augustus) his stepson by Livia, as his heir. Tiberius had proven himself a powerful military commander, an able politician, and a pious and restrained man, and though he had a penchant for gloominess and had quarrelled several times with Octavian, indicating that he did not want the responsibilities that would come with being his heir, in the end in 4 AD he accepted. Octavian was probably wise in his choice, as his other potential heirs were not especially able, and after he had named Tiberius his heir, he began gradually transferring his powers, including his tribunician and proconsular authority, to the younger man.

10 years later, on August 19th, 14 AD, Octavian died. It has been alleged by several of his ancient biographers that he was poisoned by his wife Livia (who is depicted as a terrifying figure in the famous novel *I, Claudius*) but the truth is unclear. Certainly he had often been in poor health, and he was 75 at the time of his death, so it is just as possible he died of natural causes. Reportedly, he told his wife and closest confidants, as he lay dying: "Have I played my part well? Then give me a round of applause, as I exit the stage". Following his death, he was deified as his adoptive father Julius Caesar had been, and he was succeeded virtually without incident by Tiberius, who took the titles of *Imperator* and *Princeps*, awarded to him by the Senate, a month later.

Chapter 14: Caesar's Legacy

"I love the name of honor, more than I fear death." - Caesar

To the dismay of the conspirators and their supporters, which had included luminaries like Cicero, the assassination of Caesar failed to restore the Republic to its former glory. Instead, the vacuum of power created a struggle amongst those closest to Caesar. The conspirators were quickly exiled, and from the chaos of Caesar's death rose a new triumvirate, headed by Octavian, Caesar's nephew and heir, Mark Antony, his staunchest ally, and Lepidus, a powerful general. Together the men purged their enemies, combining to defeat Brutus and Cassius at the Battle of Phillipi in October of 42 B.C. Antony's most famous rival, Cicero, was hunted down attempting to flee, and after he was murdered, Antony had his hands and head nailed to the Rostra in the Forum.

Having defeated Caesar's conspirators, Octavian and Antony turned upon each other. With Antony controlling the eastern part of the Roman Empire, he began a famous relationship with Cleopatra. Octavian's decisive victory at the Battle of Actium in 30 B.C. ensured his victory, and after Antony and Cleopatra committed suicide, the politically calculating Octavian had Caesarion, Caesar's lone son, killed. Octavian, of course, would become the first of many Roman emperors over the next 500 years. Octavian would become Caesar Augustus, and the Republic of Rome never saw another dawn.

Love him or hate him, there is no doubt that Caesar was a remarkable man, and one who changed the course of world history for ever. In addition to the fact that his heir and his heir's descendants went on to rule over one of the greatest Empires the world has ever known, much of which was conquered and consolidated by Caesar himself, his influence is still felt in many aspects of our daily life. Caesar's name is still synonymous with power, and he continues to be one of history's most famous men, if not the most famous. The West also has Caesar to thank for the fact that the calendar consists of 365 days, with an extra day every four years.

Like Alexander in the centuries before Caesar's time, Caesar became the man every leader aspired to be, both politically and militarily. Over 2,000 years after his death, Caesar is still considered one of history's greatest generals, and it's easy to understand why. He was a brilliant strategist, and unmatched tactician who defeated virtually every enemy he ever encountered. He never lost a campaign, and his roll-call of triumphs, including in Spain, Gaul, Italy, Greece, Egypt, and Numydia, eclipses most if not all great generals. Moreover, Caesar was a soldier's soldier, never afraid to take up a sword himself when his men needed to see their general the most, as he did at the Sabis, at Pharsalus, and at Munda. It would take nearly 2,000 years before generals aimed to emulate anyone other than Caesar, and that man, Napoleon, had aimed to emulate Caesar.

Ironically, European royalty across the continent took his name as an imperial title, even though Caesar himself never was and never considered himself a royal. He had simple tastes in most things, and was never given to the excesses that plagued so many of his noble contemporaries or his successors – indeed, the only accusations of vice that were ever levied against him were the ones of having had a homosexual relationship with the King of Bythinia, when he was barely in his twenties. Ever the populist, he seems to have generally cared for the common people – both his veterans, who were richly rewarded for their services, and the "mob" of Rome itself which, usually so fickle, was so enamored with him that they were willing to cast their support behind Antony and Octavian purely because they promised justice for Caesar's murder.

No doubt he was proud, perhaps even arrogant, but then, given his achievements, he had reason to be. It is said that, while still in his teens, during a visit to Spain Caesar was shown a statue of that other great conqueror, Alexander the Great of Macedon. The story has it that Caesar was severely upset by this forcible reminder of Alexander's triumphs, for he had already reached an age at which the Macedonian King had already succeeded in subjugating all of Greece, and Caesar still had precious few achievements to his name. Though Alexander's empire was vaster at its pinnacle, it was divided upon his death. The empire Caesar forged would last over 500 more years.

Of course, the legacy of the most famous Roman has endured far longer.

Chapter 15: Cleopatra's Legacy

Despite her own personal successes, Cleopatra's legacy was a ruinous one: her line extinguished, and her once independent (if subservient) kingdom reduced to a province governed directly from Rome. She had become mistress, in turn, to two of the most powerful men in the world, loved them in her own unique fashion, but betrayed one of them – Antony – in his gravest moment of peril. She was ruthless, strong-willed, arrogant in many respects, foolish in a great many others, and her political and military career, once she stepped out of the confines of Egypt, was a fiasco. Yet she was a remarkable woman for all that – anyone who has herself smuggled in a carpet past her rival's guards in order to snatch a crown from their fingers deserves admiration. Beautiful, reckless, cruel, and wanton – she was everything her enemies in Rome decried her as, but she was also ambitious, loyal, headstrong, and in many ways, wise beyond her years. Not the perfect woman, perhaps, but a great one.

Due to the tumultuous life she lived, Cleopatra remains a relevant and potent symbol as a strong-willed, independent woman who came to dominate two of the most powerful men of her age. And of course, much of the intrigue surrounding Cleopatra is a result of the mystique and uncertainty of her life and times, not to mention her very foreign religion and lifestyle. Though she died in the 1st century B.C., historians and archaeologists continue to search for her royal palace (presumed to have fallen under the sea after an earthquake) and even her burial chambers. Regardless, it can be safely assumed that people will still be talking about Cleopatra for many years to come.

Chapter 16: Antony's Legacy

After Antony's death, he was subjected to damnatio memoriae, ("damnation of the memories") by Octavian, and ironically it was Cicero's son, Cicero Minor, who had the satisfaction of announcing Antony's death to the Senate. Almost all images of Antony were destroyed, and most of his male children murdered (as were Cleopatra's sons). His daughters lived on, however, and some went on to be the mothers and grandmothers of emperors, but no members of the gens Antonia could ever legally carry the first name Marcus again.

Still, news of Antony's death was not greeted with jubilation, despite Octavian's smear campaign – after all, he had died "Roman". In the end, his premature death smacks of waste, as does much of his life. He was a man of undoubted talent, ambition and ability, and he lived in a time where such virtues could be a pathway to undying glory. Yet he was also vain, headstrong, and vicious – a drunkard, a gambler, and, as history will always best remember him, a fool for his women.

Chapter 17: Augustus's Legacy

Portrait of Augustus wearing a gorgoneion on a three layered sardonyx cameo, circa 14 A.D.

Octavian may have asked if he had played his part well, but there's no doubt he knew the answer to the question. In less than five decades, he had gradually taken over what had proudly and defiantly been a Republic for over 500 years, ready to kill any man who even considered putting on the trappings of monarchy, and turned it into an Empire. And of course, the political entity he created would go on to become one of the greatest Empires in the history of mankind, and its most famous.

Furthermore, as subsequent Roman emperors would prove time and again, having absolute power doesn't make it easy to harness and control it. Few Roman emperors sustained any semblance of popularity during their reign, and Augustus's immediate successors (especially Tiberius, Caligula, and Nero) are better known for their ineptitude and outright insanity in Caligula's case. It took unrivaled political skill to peacefully transform the Roman Republic into the Roman Empire, but it may have taken even more to maintain universal popularity while actually governing.

As history has recorded, Augustus was Rome's most famous emperor because he was its most capable. In addition to completing the political changes within Rome itself, he somehow managed to simultaneously stretch the Roman Empire's borders to previously unreached size while also establishing what came to be known as the Pax Romana ("Roman Peace"), a nearly two century long era of peace on the European continent that has not been matched since. As the history of Europe has demonstrated again and again since the collapse of Rome in 476 A.D., managing to maintain stability across Europe may have been Augustus's most amazing feat.

Though his public boast – and a true one, at that – was that he found Rome made of bricks, and left her made of marble, his last private words are infinitely more touching, and tell us far more about his character than all the official monuments and inscriptions telling of his triumphs that still litter Rome and much of Europe and Northern Africa. Did he play his part well? In all likelihood, he played it better than anyone else could have ever done.

Bibliography

In addition to Caesar's commentaries, Readers interested in learning more about Caesar & Cleopatra should consult Plutarch's biographies of Caesar and Mark Antony, as well as Suetonius's *De Vita Caesarum*. Those interested in more modern reading should refer to Stacy Schiff's excellent *Cleopatra*, or Adrian Goldsworthy's *Antony and Cleopatra*.

Readers interested in knowing more about Mark Antony from contemporary sources should consult Plutarch's Life of Antony, Caesar's De Bello Gallico, and Cicero's (undoubtedly biased) Philippics. For a more modern take on his life, readers are advised to try Patricia Southern's comprehensive Mark Antony: A Life.

Readers interested in knowing more about Augustus can consult his ancient biographers Cassius Dio and Suetonius, as well as his own autobiography the *Res Gestae Divi Augusti*, all of which are available in print or for free as part of the public domain online. For a more modern take, see Anthony Everitt's *Augustus: The Life of Rome's First Emperor*.

Printed in Great Britain
by Amazon